Resume Objective Statements
and Professional Summaries

Gary W. Capone

Palladian International, LLC
105-A Lew Dewitt Blvd. Suite 197
Waynesboro, VA 22980

ISBN-13: 978-1463768140

ISBN-10: 1463768141

Contents

Introduction

The most important and difficult section of a resume to write is the introduction. Despite this, the typical resume writing book only provides a chapter or two on how to write a strong, powerful and impressive introductory section. This book is different. It is entirely focused on objective statements and professional summaries, and it is the only book of its kind. This is also the book you need to gain an edge on your competition.

A resume is a sales document. It needs to sell a hiring manager on your potential and persuade the hiring manager to want to learn more about you. Successfully selling a hiring manage on you requires grabbing their attention and making a very strong first impression. Hiring managers typically spend 15 to 30 seconds on each resume before deciding to discard it or to continue reading. You need to capture their attention during this time. The first impression you make is absolutely critical, otherwise, you won't get a chance to make a second impression.

There are a lot of books on resume writing. Many are great resources. They provide advice and techniques on every aspect of a resume. With this approach, the typical resume writing book has only a chapter or two on how to write an introduction. This is inadequate, and most job seekers struggle as a result. This isn't to say these books aren't valuable. They are important resources for job seekers. They just don't provide the level of detail and instruction needed about what I consider to be the most critical element of a resume.

I set out to write a book that would provide job seekers with a depth of instruction that is unequaled. A book that doesn't just give a few pieces of advice, but instead gives job seekers the tools and knowledge to confidently and effectively write a powerful introductory section.

My recommendations, advice and techniques are based on years of assessing, writing and studying resumes. I've screened tens of thousands of resumes as an executive recruiter. This has shown me that most resumes have weak and unimpressive introductions. That is if the resume has an introduction – many resumes fail to include an introductory section. Even worse, many job seekers start with an introduction that hurts their chances of getting an interview.

I've always known that writing a resume is a critical skill. In recruiting, it is important to package a candidate to make the best impression. To ensure that I could write the best possible resumes, I decided to study resumes. My background is very analytical. In school, I completed Mechanical Engineering and Accounting degrees, simultaneously. I've worked in both fields and have always been drawn to analyzing and improving processes.

I set out to look at resume writing as a process that could be optimized. The first step was to study resumes and develop some hard data on what works and what doesn't.

Over the years, I have conducted a number of resume research studies, covering different industries and different aspects of the resumes. Although I was a pretty good resume writer when I started this research, it still taught me a number of things. I developed guidelines for resume structures, length, formatting, the content of a resume and other details. I can quote statistics. For example, more than 25% of all resumes do not include a single accomplishment (a very big mistake).

I also got very good at picking out the qualities of a resume introduction that make it effective. I am going to teach you how to do this, and help you write a powerful introduction that will get attention.

This book is not just a bunch of resume writing theory. I don't think you can learn to write an effective introduction without seeing examples. Because of this, I have included numerous examples of objective statements and professional summaries. Each example includes an assessment and recommendations for improvements. In many cases, I even provide a rewritten version showing exactly what I would change.

These examples will teach you how to write a more effective resume introduction. You will learn to avoid common mistakes, and incorporate the best practices. These are the best practices I have identified after studying thousands of resumes.

What Is a Resume Introduction?

A resume introduction is a section at the top of a resume that motivates the reader to want to read the rest of the resume. The introduction should create a strong first impression. There are two primary forms of the introduction, the objective statement and the professional summary.

An objective statement conveys the career goal of the job seeker. This is important because a hiring manager needs to know how to assess the resume. Hiring managers, particularly the resume screener who will be the first person at a company to read your resume, often are hiring for a wide range of positions. To assess your resume, the reader needs to know what assessment criteria to use. An objective can answer this question quickly, so the hiring manager can focus on the content of the resume.

The professional summary focuses on the strongest selling points of the job seeker. It can emphasize a limited portion of a job seeker's career, or try to cover it all. The goal is to create a strong first impression about the value the job seeker offers. A well-written professional summary can be the most important element of the resume, and dramatically improve the effectiveness of the resume.

Although there are a few resumes with both an objective statement and professional summary, these are typically alternatives. In most situations, a professional summary will be more effective. It is important to know which option is better for your specific situation, and this book explains how to choose the best option for you.

Book Organization

The book begins with a discussion of resume structures. It is important to understand how the introduction fits with the other sections of the resume. This allows the development of a good organization for a resume. Although the introduction is a critical element and essential to make a strong first impression, it is only one component. You need to have the right sections following the introduction to maximize the effectiveness.

After the chapter on resume sections, the book looks at the differences between objective statements and professional summaries. Both are examined in great detail in the book. I prefer resumes with a professional summary over an objective statement. Despite this, it is important for you to understand how each works and decide which is best for you.

Chapters 3 through 7 focus on objective statements. These five chapters will teach you how to write an effective objective, and show you how to improve your current objective. Numerous examples are provided.

Chapters 8 though 12 focus on professional summaries. Like the chapters on objectives, you will learn how to write an effective professional summary step-by-step. There are a lot of examples to help you see what works and what doesn't.

Finally, chapters 13 through 16 cover other design aspects of your resume introduction. Advice for customizing your resume and recommendations for formatting your professional summary are provided. The book concludes with lists of verbs and adjectives. These chapters will help you regardless of the style of introduction you choose.

You've taken a great step to improve your resume. The techniques you will learn from this book and apply in your resume will help you maximize the effectiveness of your resume!

Chapter 1
Resume Structure

There are three primary structures for resumes: chronological, functional and hybrid. Chronological resumes are organized around the work history of the job seeker. Functional resumes are organized around skills. The hybrid resume incorporates elements of both.

Almost all professionals should use a chronological structure. Chronological resumes are the most common and hiring managers are most familiar with this structure. There are times to use a different format, but for the majority of people, the chronological format is best. Unless you have a very good reason to use a different format, stick with the chronological.

Chronological resumes make the job seeker's work experience the focus of the resume's main section. Jobs are listed in reverse chronological order, with the most recent job first. Chronological resumes do a good job of showing a person's career progression. This is an extremely important element of your background that hiring managers assess, and the chronological resume focuses on conveying this information.

Resume Sections

A typical chronological resume contains three or four sections. Most resumes start with an introduction section, comprised of either an objective statement or professional summary. The next two sections are typically the work experience and the education sections. Many job seekers then add additional sections with information important to their specific career field. Each section is designed to present a specific type of information.

The common resume sections are listed below. A typical resume will include a few of these, but not all. For example, most resumes choose to include either an objective statement or a professional summary, but not both. Most resumes will include a total of 3 to 6 sections.

Objective Statement – An objective statement is a type of introduction for the resume. It is designed to convey to the reader the types of jobs the job seeker is pursuing. This allows the reader to consider the job seeker for the appropriate position without having to guess. When a hiring manager does not know what job a resume is for, the hiring manager must take time to read the resume and determine the right career field. They then have to guess. For job seekers changing career fields, this can lead to confusion. The faster the hiring manager identifies the job a person is pursuing, the faster they can start assessing the resume.

Professional Summary – A professional summary is another type of introduction for the resume. It provides highlights of the job seeker's experience, skills and accomplishments to demonstrate the potential value the job seeker offers. A good professional summary will generate a lot of interest in the candidate and cause the hiring manager to want to learn more. A professional summary is often the strongest and most effective sales pitch for the job seeker.

Work Experience Section – The job seeker's employment history is presented in reverse chronological order. Each job listing should contain the employer name, job title, start and end dates, a summary of the responsibilities of the role and several noteworthy accomplishments. This section should form the majority of the resume.

Education Section – The education section presents the job seeker's formal education and additional workshops, training and certifications that are significant.

Skills Section – Technical skills are an essential requirement for many fields. Even in non-technical roles, there are often skills that are essential for success. Creating a skills section can be a great way to list important skills. This section also provides an opportunity to add some keywords you want to include in your resume. A skills section will often be placed at or near the end of the resume.

Languages – Speaking multiple languages is a skill valuable to many companies. International firms often consider language skills a key selling point. It is also important for leadership positions where a significant percentage of the workforce is likely to have limited English speaking skills. Language skills are important enough to set off in a separate section. When listing language skills, it is important to qualify the skill. Just putting "Spanish" on a resume does not mean much. Did you pick up a language tape and listen to it in the car yesterday, or are you a native speaker? Provide some assessment of your language skills to clarify your skill level.

Projects – For consulting, project management, and other fields, providing a section with a project listing is a good way to show your skills and accomplishments. The project list should include the details of each project, including your role, the scope of the project and the results achieved.

Other Sections – There are a number of other possible resume sections that some job seekers may consider. Often these are industry or skill specific. Others will attempt to highlight information that would otherwise be buried in another section. For example, some job seekers will break their education section into two sections, one with formal education and another focused on continuing education and certifications. When choosing sections for your resume, consider adding sections that provide a focus on the elements most important to the hiring manager.

Resume Order

The order of your resume will be dependent upon two things: your most significant skills, experiences and accomplishments, and the requirements and expectations of the hiring manager.

For job seekers with a limited amount of experience, your education will be the biggest selling point. In this case, you will want to put your education near the top of your resume. A good structure would be:

Professional Summary

Education

Work Experience

Over time, your work experience will become more significant, and your education will become less important. As this happens, you will change this order so your education is at the bottom, and your work experience is above it. There are no hard-and-fast rules when to make this switch. Generally, you will want to do this sometime five to ten years after you graduate with your undergraduate degree. The new structure will be:

Professional Summary

Work Experience

Education

Skills

If you graduated from a top school with a very highly regarded degree, you may choose to keep your education at the top of your resume a little longer. If you graduated from a less well known school and took a position with a very well respected employer, you might choose to move your work experience to the top almost immediately. The key is to present first the information that will be the most eye catching.

Resume Length

Your resume needs to be concise. A hiring manager will not spend a lot of time reading each resume, especially in the first screening step. In fact, the hiring manager may spend as little as 15 to 30 seconds on your resume before making a decision to reject you.

In this brief time, a person can only read a little. Most people read between 200 and 250 words per minute. That means less than 125 words can be read in the first 30 seconds. Most candidates will be rejected after the hiring manager reads as few as 50 words of the resume. In this time, the reader will focus on the information at the top of the resume, and the items that are larger, bolded and indented will draw the most attention. These formatting techniques guide the reader to what is important. Information that appears unimportant due to the formatting choices will be skipped.

The actual content that gets read is often the first line of the resume, the company name and job title for the most recent two or three jobs you have held, your degree and a couple of major bullet points from within your work experience. If you don't capture the reader's attention with this information and make a strong impression, you will be rejected. There could be a detail in your resume that would interest a hiring manager, but because the hiring manager doesn't read that detail, you end up in the rejected pile. The reader probably has more than a hundred resumes to read and will not spend a lot of time on resumes that don't look really close to what they want.

Fortunately, you can influence what elements of your resume are read. Designing your resume properly will lead the reader to the most important details first. A key strategy in this design is the effective use of an introductory section. This book will help you learn to emphasize and draw the reader to your most impressive selling points.

There is a built in conflict when determine the best length for a resume. First, you want to include as many skills, experiences and accomplishments as possible to impress hiring managers. Second, you want to focus your resume on your core sales pitch and keep it as short and concise as possible. You must balance the two goals.

For many job seekers, packing their resume with as many details as possible wins out. They try to list every skill and experience from their background. This is understandable. It can be very difficult to know what will be the most important detail to a hiring manager, so job seekers throw everything into their resumes.

Every detail you provide in your resume competes with the other details for the attention of the reader. Providing a lot of extra "low priority" details will distract the reader away from your key selling points, and may lead to your being rejected before your key selling points are even read.

How do you balance these competing priorities? You should focus the attention of the reader on the most important details by creating a really strong introduction. This should be between 75 and 150 words. You can then provide a lot more detail further down in your resume.

Consider an operations manager seeking a position in a plastic injection molding facility. The job seeker will want to show his leadership, technical skill and accomplishments with managing injection molding operations at the top of the resume. The job seeker can then, much later in the resume, give details of his experience with other processes and materials. The focus of the resume becomes injection molding management, and the other experiences become minor details. This organization will allow a hiring manager to determine almost immediately that the job seeker is qualified technically for an injection molding management position.

Now, consider what most job seekers do. They want to show the full range of their experience to "really impress" the hiring manager. They also want to create a generic resume that can be used for a wide range of industries. To do this, the job seeker lists all of the materials and processes they have managed at the top of the resume. This does two things. First, the additional details distract the reader from what is important – the injection molding experience. Second, by placing the other experiences on equal footing with the injection molding experience, the job seeker dilutes the impression they make in this area – they end up looking less like an injection molding expert and are more likely to be passed over for injection molding management positions.

For most career fields, the overall length of your resume should be between 400 and 900 words on one to two pages and it should not be more two pages. (Note: There are a few exceptions to this rule. For example, federal positions and some academic roles require longer resumes.) For recent college graduates, your resume should be one page. Sometime in your first five to ten years of experience, you will need to add a second page. Even with forty years of experience, you should stick to two pages. Remember, the reader is only going to give your resume a limited amount of time. Adding more content will not cause them to read more. It will only cause them to read lower priority information at the expense of your top selling points.

Chapter 2
Objective Statements and
Professional Summaries

There are two primary forms of introductory sections – the objective statement and the professional summary. Neither is a required element of a resume, but either can improve the effectiveness of a resume.

In rare cases, job seekers have provided both objective statements and professional summaries. This is possible and acceptable, but usually not recommended. An effective professional summary will include enough information to convey the job seeker's objective, even if the objective is not overtly stated. If an objective statement is added to a resume with a professional summary, it is usually redundant information that can be eliminated.

An introductory section, although not a required element of a resume, is extremely important to a resume's effectiveness. Without an introduction, the hiring manager must read the bulk of the resume to understand the job seeker's background. This may sound like a good thing. Job seekers want their resumes read completely so that all of their experiences, skills and accomplishments are conveyed. Unfortunately, hiring managers do not try to read and understand every detail on a resume. A typical hiring manager will spend 15 to 30 seconds on a resume before making the first decision to either reject the candidate or to keep reading. In 15 to 30 seconds, the average person will only read 50 to 100 words. After that limited scan, many candidates are rejected.

The downfall of many candidates is the selection of the 50 to 100 words that are read. In a recent resume study, the average resume was found to be around 750 words. That means many candidates are rejected after less than 15% of their resume is read. The job seeker doesn't get to pick which 15% is read. The hiring manager will skip around, scanning different sections and looking for the most significant elements. Unfortunately, if your resume does not have exceptional formatting, the hiring manager may be drawn to elements that do not do the best job of selling your potential.

Even worse, if the hiring manager does not know what job you are pursuing, the hiring manager may spend some or all of that first 15 to 30 seconds just trying to figure out what job to consider you for. If this is the case, your resume will get a very limited opportunity to impress the hiring manager after he or she figures out what you want.

There is a solution to this dilemma: provide an introduction that allows the hiring manager to better utilize the first 30 seconds they are scanning your resume. Objective statements and professional summaries do just this.

An objective statement can be a great way to start your resume. It provides a clear statement of the type of job you are pursuing so the hiring manager doesn't waste any time trying to figure out what you want. This allows the hiring manager to immediately begin assessing you for your desired position.

A professional summary takes the objective statement to another level. It is like a mini resume within a resume. A good professional summary will include the most significant elements from the resume in one place. It summarizes the job seeker's experience, skills, accomplishments and education. It even conveys the objective of the job seeker.

So, which is better, an objective statement or professional summary? A resume with a well written professional summary often provides the more impressive presentation of a job seeker's potential. This can make a tremendous impact. Developing a strong professional summary is a lot more work than an objective, but it is usually worth it. An objective can be effective in some instances, but for most job seekers, the professional summary will be better. So, does this mean you should skip the chapters on objective statements? No, they will help you better understand the perspective of a hiring manager screening resumes. Even if you choose to add a professional summary, you will still need the summary to convey your career goals. The chapters on objective statements provide a good foundation.

Chapter 3
Objective Statements

An objective statement can clarify your goals and the type of position you are pursuing. This can make it much easier for a hiring manager to assess your resume, but if done poorly; an objective statement can make a very bad impression. It all depends on what you write. Your resume is first and foremost a sales pitch for why you should be interviewed and hired. Your objective statement lists what you want – your desired job. This puts the purposes of your resume and your objective statement in conflict. For your resume to be effective, it needs to focus on the hiring manager's goals, not yours.

So, does that mean a resume should not have an objective? No, objective statements can be very important and effective elements of a resume. It is essential that you convey the type of position you are pursuing for the hiring manager to be able to assess your resume. Unfortunately, most objective statements are ineffective and some are major detractors, hurting the job seekers' chances. You have to have the right objective, and incorporate it into your resume effectively.

The first step in writing an effective objective statement is to understand how the reader of your resume will use it. The person who will find your objective the most valuable is the first person who reads your resume at a company. This resume screener is often a recruiter at the company. They are responsible for reviewing all resumes that are submitted. This person will have multiple positions they are trying to fill at the company in completely different fields.

The resume screener must assess your resume. To assess your resume, they must know what standards to assess it against. Every position is likely to have different qualifications required, so knowing what job to assess your resume against is essential before the screener can even start reading your resume.

A resume screener will determine how to assess your resume several different ways. One of the easiest is to look at the job you applied for. If you applied for a particular position, there's a pretty good chance that position is a goal of yours. That is your objective, and the resume screener will have that knowledge before they open your resume.

Every resume does not get submitted to a single position, and your background may be suitable for a range of roles. A recruiter will recognize this, and may consider you for other positions. You may submit your resume online to a job board, or give it to an associate for consideration at a company. In these cases, the reader will have nothing to go on except what is in the resume. This makes it essential to show what career you are pursuing.

If the resume screener does not know what job to consider you for when they open your resume, they are likely to use your last position as a guide. They will assume you want to do something similar to what you have been doing. For most people, this would be a correct assumption. For individuals who are changing career fields, the most-recent job can be misleading, and for new graduates, there is no history to use as a guide.

Individuals in these situations, who are just entering a new career field, need to work harder to make it easy to understand what jobs they are pursuing. This is where an objective becomes helpful.

If you have worked in one career field for a long time and are looking for a job in the same career field, you do not need an objective statement. A hiring manager reading your resume will assume you want to keep doing what you have been doing.

Chapter 4
Types of Objective Statements

There are several different types of objective statements, with each relating to the type of information being conveyed. An objective can focus on the career field, industry, type of work or location. Some focus on personal desires. Objective statements can be direct and to the point, or they can be very lengthy and detailed. Not all of these options are effective. Some will help you land a job, and some will hurt.

Career Field: Most objective statements focus on the career field of the job seeker. They provide a job title or selection of titles the job seeker is pursuing. These are typically very short objectives, and some of the most effective. They convey a single piece of information, the job you are seeking, and do it very efficiently.

Industry: Some job seekers want to focus their search in a particular industry, and use an objective to reinforce this goal. Usually, this is unnecessary. If you apply to a company, you will be pursuing your industry goals. There is no need to tell the hiring manager about your industry preference on your resume. If you are posting your resume on a job board, or applying to a third party recruiter who works in multiple industries, listing your industry goals will be more valuable.

Type of Work: Although the job titles listed in your objective will give a strong indication of the type of work you are seeking, there are other details you may want to convey. You can include details about the primary emphasis of the position. For example, some job seekers will pursue turnaround opportunities. These are situations where an organization is performing very poorly, and the company is seeking a person to rapidly change and improve the organization. This is a vastly different situation than a company that is performing very well.

Location: When posting your resume online, it is important to convey your geographic flexibility. If you are open to relocation, there will be many more opportunities available to you. Fortunately, most job posting boards offer the ability to set your relocation preferences. Although your location may be important to you and employers, it is rare that this information is valuable in an objective statement.

Personal Desires: There are job seekers who put personal interests and desires in their objective statement. These can include commuting distances, specific benefits, and other details that the job seeker wants. This is a mistake. It distracts the reader from your qualifications, and creates a bad impression. Everyone knows that you are seeking a job in order to obtain something. You don't need to tell the hiring manager that the job needs to benefit you. Placing personal desires in an objective statement usually makes the job seeker appear self-centered, demanding and unprofessional. Stay away from putting this information on your resume.

In addition to the types of information included in an objective, the overall length of the objective statement is also important. Some job seekers pack more into their objective than they do their cover letter or the rest of their resume. This is a huge mistake. The goal of your resume is to make a strong enough impression to motivate the reader to want to interview you. Other than indicating what job you are pursuing, your objective does nothing to achieve this goal. In fact, it distracts the reader from the information that might motivate them to want to speak with you. This makes it essential to keep the length of an objective to a minimum.

Chapter 5
Are Objective Statements Necessary?

A hiring manager must have a way of determining what job you should be considered for. This is essential. You cannot be considered without some frame of reference. There are job seekers who try to be all things to all people. This is a mistake. If you generalize yourself enough, you will ensure that you are overlooked for every job.

Consider a job seeker who has worked in three career fields over his career. He's held two or three jobs in each career field. In total, he's worked in eight different positions. He then designs his resume to present all eight of these positions equally. His resume must limit the amount of detail about each position. Now a hiring manager reviews his resume considering him for a position similar to one of the eight jobs the candidate has held. The resume demonstrates very little depth of expertise in this area, and instead shows a wide range of experiences. The resume ends up creating an impression with the hiring manager that the job seeker does not have much skill or experience in the one job the hiring manager is trying to fill. The candidate gets rejected in favor of more specialized candidates.

Now, consider another candidate with a similar background. This candidate focuses their resume on one job. There is a great depth of experience related to that job. For all the other positions, the job seeker has held, the resume highlights important experiences and accomplishments that relate to the one job the candidate is seeking. The result is a very focused resume. When a hiring manager reads the resume, it will make a much stronger impression.

The job you are focusing your resume on is one element of your resume's theme. Your resume needs to have a strong theme that runs throughout the resume. This theme should be reinforced in your cover letter, and provide a foundation for your interview answers. A good theme will tie the job you are seeking to your experience, education, skills and accomplishments. Together, this will create the overall impression of who you are. Without a coherent theme, you are less likely to be invited to an interview and less likely to get hired.

Your objective statement can help create the theme you desire. It starts your resume with a statement focusing your goals. Objective statements are just one way to create this impression. There are other techniques you can use to achieve the same thing. For now, we will focus on just the objective statement. Later, we will review other techniques when we look at professional summaries.

Chapter 6
Elements of an Effective Objective Statement

An effective objective statement will help focus your resume while being very brief and concise. The shorter the objective, the better. You need to sell a hiring manager on your potential. Although conveying the type of job you are pursuing is essential, your objective does nothing to demonstrate your value to a company. Your objective is about what you want, but your resume is designed to sell your potential to an employer. What you want is of little concern to an employer, so make sure your objective is as short as possible.

Being concise is important, but so is being specific. Too many objective statements don't say anything. They are terrible. For example, a common objective statement found on many resumes is similar to the following: "Seeking an exciting opportunity utilizing my skills to the benefit of the company."

I hate reading objectives like this. They are a complete waste of time. This objective does nothing to limit the search. Essentially, the job seeker is saying that they want a job where they have the ability to do the job. In other words, if the company thinks the job seeker will be a benefit to the company, then the job seeker wants the job.

An objective can be useful on a resume if it helps establish a strong theme for the resume, and helps the hiring manager know what job to consider the job seeker for. The generic objective above fails in both cases. It is a waste of space and a distraction.

A better objective statement will provide a specific career field or job that is being sought. It will convey this in a direct and concise manner.

Your objective statement can include some text explaining that you are providing an objective statement. The most common way job seekers will do this is to start with the word "Objective" and then list their objective afterward. For example:

Objective: Production Manager or Plant Manager

This leaves no question what job the candidate is pursuing. It is direct and very easy to understand. With an objective like this on the top of a resume, it will only take a second to understand what job to assess the job seeker for.

Some job seekers will omit the word "Objective" as a title and just provide the job titles that they are seeking. For example, the first line of the resume could be:

Production Manager or Plant Manager

This can be effective. It is very direct and concise, and the statement makes it clear the type of jobs the candidate is pursuing.

Other job seekers incorporate the objective into a professional summary section. This style attempts to integrate the objective into the resume so that it flows smoothly and does not distract the reader from the rest of the resume. This type of summary section will typically start with a branding statement, and transition into the objective. For example:

Highly accomplishment production manager with 15 years of experience improving processes and cutting costs, seeking production and plant management opportunities.

This style focuses on the job seeker's sales pitch, but includes details of the individual's goals. It is a little more subtle than the overt objective statement, but can still be very effective.

Another technique is to omit the "seeking" portion of the objective statement. It is possible to list the job title being sought as a title of the summary section. This provides a branding statement with the first words of the resume. The title makes it clear the resume is geared to that particular career field. For example, you could use the job title "Production Manager" as the title of the resume:

> *Production Manager: Successful leader skilled at implementing lean manufacturing improvements, cutting costs and delivering bottom line results*

This example conveys a clear goal of working in production management, even though it never says overtly that this is the objective. Using Production Manager as a title to the resume implies the career field the job seeker is seeking. Using this technique, you can provide a very direct and concise objective while staying focused on selling your potential to the hiring manager.

Using a job title as the title of your resume is one method of creating a professional summary for your resume. A professional summary is a section that provides highlights of your background to get a hiring manager excited about you. It pulls all of your most impressive selling points into one section. Using the job title establishes the area of focus for your resume, and eliminates the need for an overt objective statement. In most cases, a professional summary section with a clear theme tailored to the needs of the company will provide a much stronger and more professional presentation than an objective statement alone.

Chapter 7
Examples of Objective Statements

The best way to understand what makes an effective objective statement is to work as a recruiter, either inside a company or at an agency, and screen thousands of resumes. After a short time, a recruiter learns what information is valuable to them. They then start to scan for that information and try to skip the information that doesn't add value.

Unfortunately, working as a recruiter, screening thousands of resumes, is not a viable plan for most job seekers. The next best thing is to simulate this experience and assess as many resumes and objective statements as possible. This chapter presents a number of objectives from actual job seekers. Picture each of these as the first line of a resume. Then assess the statement, and determine if it adds value and creates a strong, professional impression. As you assess the objective statements, consider the following questions:

- Is the statement sufficiently specific?
- Do you know what the job seeker is looking for?
- Is the statement short and concise?
- Would you read the entire statement if you had 200 resumes to screen?
- Does the statement create a professional image?
- Do you want to learn more about the job seeker?

As you review the objective statements, an assessment is provided of each. The assessment is followed by an improved version of the objective.

> *Objective: General Manager in an established and successful business.*

Assessment: The objective is vague. A general manager position covers a wide range of career fields and industries and does little to narrow the search. Also, the job seeker indicates they want an established successful business, and this adds little value. Is the job seeker really going to turn down a position from a company that is a start up or a company that is currently struggling? More importantly, the statement shifts hiring manager's thought process to a question of whether their business measures up to the job seeker's expectations. This distracts the hiring manager from the job seeker's qualifications.

Improvement: Provide an industry, and drop the "established and successful business" part. For example, "Objective: Distribution Center General Manager."

> *Position Targets: Director of Lean Manufacturing, Continuous Improvement Manager, Value Stream Manager, Lean Manufacturing Champion, Process Improvement Manager, Continuous Improvement Leader, and Process Improvement Consultant.*

Assessment: This objective is very specific but too long and not very effective. The job seeker wants a role where he can be in a leadership position improving manufacturing processes with lean methodologies. He does this by listing a lot of job titles. The objective is too long and needs to be shorter.

Improvement: Instead of listing a bunch of job titles, list a career field. For example, "Objective: Manufacturing leadership role championing lean and other continuous improvement programs."

> *OBJECTIVE: Obtain a challenging leadership position applying lean management and creative problem solving skills with a growing company to achieve ideal utilization of its resources and maximization of profits.*

Assessment: This is way too wordy and packed with non-essential information. Every job is responsible for "achieving ideal utilization of its resources and maximization of profits." This should be cut out. Instead, the job seeker could have written "Objective: A challenging leadership position applying lean principles." This would be better. Unfortunately, it's still too vague. We don't know what career field the job seeker is pursuing. Are they a manufacturing manager, hospital administrator, logistics professional or something else?

Improvement: Add a specific career field and eliminate the non-essential elements. Using a hospital administrator as an example: "Objective: Lead hospital performance improvement initiatives with lean management practices."

> *PROFESSIONAL OBJECTIVE: To progress in my career with an organization that will utilize my Management, Supervision & Administrative skills to benefit the growth and success of the company.*

Assessment: There is nothing in this that indicates what career field the job seeker wants. Listing Management, Supervision and Administrative covers a huge breadth of careers. Also, the objective includes the overused theme "to benefit the growth and success of the company." This type of language appears in a lot of objectives. It essentially says that the candidate does not want a job where he will harm the company.

Improvement: This is tough. There's little to go on. We only know that the candidate wants something with management, supervision and administration. To improve this, we have to pick a career for the job seeker that has these three elements. Using a department manager in a retail store as an example: "Objective: Department manager in a retail store."

> Objective: I am currently looking for a fulltime position in an environment that offers an exciting challenge, increased benefits for my family, and the opportunity to help the company grow efficiently and productively

Assessment: The first thing that jumps out is the phrase "increased benefits for my family." This is undoubtedly a true statement, and the individual may have a real need for improved benefits. Unfortunately, this is an example where the candidate is too focused on his needs, and not selling his potential. There is nothing in this objective that is helpful to a hiring manager.

Improvement: There is nothing in this objective that provides any value. The best option would be to delete this objective completely and start over.

> Objective: Director of Operations/General Manager

Assessment: This is direct and to the point. It is not very specific, as these job titles appear in a wide range of industries. Although it is too vague to be useful, the statement is short enough that it is unlikely to be a major distraction.

Improvement: All that is needed here is something indicating the career field. Let's assume the job seeker works in the hospitality industry. Example: "Objective: Hotel General Manager or Director of Operations."

> *Employment Objective: My goal is to become associated with a company where I can utilize my skills and abilities to gain experience while enhancing the company's productivity and reputation.*

Assessment: This says nothing. The job seeker wants a job he is qualified to do and where he will add value to the company. The purpose of an objective is to tell the reader what jobs the job seeker wants to do, can do and will add value doing. Saying your objective is to get a job is redundant. It's a resume, and this is implied. Unfortunately, this style of objective is very common. It is just a sentence meant to sound good with no substance. Hiring managers are smart enough to recognize this. There is no magic phrase that you can put on a resume that will lead to an interview. Hiring managers will only be impressed by your experience, education, skills and accomplishments.

Improvement: There is nothing in this objective that provides any value. The best option would be to delete this objective completely and start over.

> *Objective: To secure a position with a stable and profitable company, where I can be a member of a team and utilize my experience to the fullest.*

Assessment: This objective is similar to the previous one. It says nothing and is essentially a long winded version of "I want a job."

Improvement: There is nothing in this objective that provides any value. The best option would be to delete this objective completely and start over.

Objective: To further my professional career with an executive level management position in a large world class company, where I can diversify my skills in another industry. Relocation desirable.

Assessment: This objective is interesting, and actually contains some substance. The individual indicates they want an executive level position. This is still too vague. There should be an indication of a specialty – operations, supply chain, accounting, human resources, sales, marketing, etc. The objective gives some other information that may be helpful. The job seeker wants to change industries, but unfortunately doesn't indicate what industry they want to go into. They also indicate a preference for large companies, and indicate that they are open to relocation. Overall, the objective is still too wordy and too vague, but at least it has a few details.

Improvement: We need to choose a career field and possibly an industry to rewrite this. It also needs to be more concise. Let's assume this is an HR exec. The candidate does not have an industry preference listed, so we will not indicate a preferred industry. Example: "Objective: Executive Human Resources role. Relocation desirable."

JOB TARGET: Permanent employment or a long-term consulting project.

Assessment: This candidate is open to anything except temp work. This may be the broadest objective yet, and one of the least valuable.

Improvement: There is nothing in this objective that provides any value. The best option would be to delete this objective completely and start over.

> OBJECTIVE: I am pursuing a career as an account manager with limited overnight travel. I am seeking to deliver my research, analytical, and presentation skills to the benefit of the company.

Assessment: This objective is specific and provides details of the career the job seeker wants. Unfortunately, the job seeker makes a horrible impression with the second sentence. He's looking for an account manager position. Essentially, this is a sales job. His most important skill should be selling, and his primary objective should be to sell. Secondarily, he should focus on relationship building, customer service and communications skills. Instead he talks about wanting to utilize his research and analytical skills. This creates an impression of a sales rep who doesn't want to sell. He has almost ensured that he will not get an interview with his objective statement.

Improvement: The job seeker has two options to fix this. First, he can emphasize sales skills. For example, "Objective: Grow sales in an account management role using my exceptional sales, relationship building and communications skills." Second, he can change his focus to a sales support role. For example, "Objective: Lead research and analysis in a sales and marketing support role, focused on identifying prospects and expanding existing customers." Either one of these options is correct. It's ultimately up to the job seeker to decide what his true goals are.

OBJECTIVE: To contribute excellent project and operations management skills and experience in an IT Service Management role.

Assessment: This is a little wordy, but other than that, pretty good. It provides an industry and a skill set that implies the career field.

Improvement: We need to simplify this objective. The career field is straightforward and just needs to tightened up. Example: "Objective: IT Services Manager"

Objective: Seeking a position in a professional office environment where my skills are valued and can benefit the organization. Ideally, I wish to focus on marketing for a growing organization preferably dealing in commercial real estate and/or land acquisitions.

Assessment: This objective starts out very vague. Many hiring managers will read the first line and skip the rest. Despite this, the job seeker does eventually get to their objective. They are very non-committal, using words like ideally and preferably. It sounds like the job seeker has a goal but is afraid of missing other opportunities as they focus on their goal. This is common. Many job seekers worry about the jobs they may pass up while pursuing others. This is a mistake. As long as the job seeker is not focused and decisive, they will struggle. The objective only serves to demonstrate that the job seeker is afraid to make a decision and is uncertain of what they want to do.

Improvement: To fix this, it needs to be shortened and focused. Example: "Objective: A marketing role in commercial real estate or land acquisitions."

> *Objective: My objective is to obtain a position as an engineering VP, director or manager, leading initiatives that utilize state-of-the-art software and/or hardware components with a creative, technology-driven organization in an environment that encourages innovative thinking, recognition, and career development. Customer interaction is desired.*

Assessment: This isn't bad. It describes the career field and industry. It even describes the type of culture and company. Unfortunately, it's too long, and it has redundant information. The job seeker wants to use state-of-the-art technology, in a technology-driven company that is innovative. These elements are likely to go together. Any organization that is technology-driven better be innovative and use state of the art technology. We can shorten this and deliver a better objective.

Improvement: Making the objective more concise and eliminating elements that are related and similar will make it more effective. Example: "Objective: Senior Management role in engineering with a technology-driven company."

> *CAREER OBJECTIVE: A challenging and rewarding Logistics / Distribution Operations Management position within the private sector where previous experience, ability, skills and a commitment to professionalism would be of value. Position should allow for continued personal and professional development.*

Assessment: This is much longer than it needs to be, and it includes too much about how the position needs to benefit the job seeker. Remember, hiring managers are not interested at this stage with what the job seeker wants. They are focused on what they want.

Improvement: Get rid of the non-essential elements. Example: "Career Objective: Logistics / Distribution Manager."

> Objective: Seeking a fulfilling position in the facility service industry that offers growth opportunities and allows me to utilize my leadership skills and experience.

Assessment: This is short and details a specific industry. Unfortunately, it doesn't say anything about the type of job.

Improvement: We need to be more specific about the job seeker's career field. The candidate mentions leadership skills, so we will assume the job seeker is a supervisor or team leader. Example: "Objective: Maintenance Service Team Leader"

> Objective: Seeking a position as Systems Engineer and support of all IT Needs.

Assessment: This is pretty good. It's direct and clearly describes the type of job the job seeker is pursuing. It's a little wordy. This may seem like nitpicking, but your resume needs to be efficient. Every non-essential word is a word a hiring manager has to read before they get to something important. In this objective statement, the job seeker more than doubles the number of words needed to convey the same information.

Improvement: This objective could be drastically shortened. Example: "Objective: IT Systems Engineer." Additionally, the job seeker may want to add something about a particular technology.

Example: "Objective: Unix/Linux Systems Engineer." This version not only has less than half the words of the original, but it also provides a technical specialty.

> *CAREER OBJECTIVE: Position as an engineer or a similar role, which offers key participation, team-oriented tasks, immediate challenges, and career opportunity.*

Assessment: This is too wordy and not specific enough. The job seeker wants an engineering position, but never indicates the type. Remember that the first person reading the resume is trying to decide what position to consider the job seeker for. Engineering covers a wide range of disciplines. Does the candidate want to be a design engineer, applications engineer, process engineer, facilities engineer, etc? In addition, the job seeker doesn't indicate the engineering discipline, such as mechanical, electrical, metallurgical, systems, chemical, etc?

Improvement: For this example, assume the engineer is an electrical engineer seeking an applications engineering position supporting a company's sales efforts. Example: "Objective: Applications engineer focused on electrical engineering."

> *Objective: Seek to work in a New Business Development role utilizing my superior knowledge, prospecting and selling abilities in the business to business arena.*

Assessment: This is pretty good. It clearly defines the position and then discusses the candidate's skills related to the position. Unlike the common "…utilizing my skills and abilities to the benefit of the company" style objective, this lists specific skills that are typically valued in business development roles.

Improvement: There are a few ways to improve this objective. We can keep the current style and rewrite it by eliminating the non-essential words. Going to an extremely, we could focus on just the job title. Example: "Objective: New Business Development." If we want to keep the skills, we could still shorten this. Example: "New Business Development: Highly skilled at B2B prospecting and selling."

If we adopt a different style, we can put more into the skills description and really develop the presentation of the job seeker's potential. Example: "New Business Development: Exceptional sales rep, highly skilled at prospecting and opening new accounts, with an established track record of beating sales quotas and growing revenues." Now, this is not a true objective statement. It is a branding or positioning statement, and would be used as the first line of a professional summary. Later in the book, we will look at professional summaries, and how they can make a very strong impression.

OBJECTIVE: Seek to work in an environment that will challenge me further, while allowing me to contribute to the success of the organization. Obtain a position that will offer me the ability to utilize my sales and work experience in a growth industry. Look forward to working with a company that delivers quality products and services, and provides me with the opportunity to meet and exceed individual sales expectations. Utilize consultative selling approach coupled with the hard work and determination as an individual contributor with minimal supervision or team selling environment. Experience with quotas ranging from 20k per month to 2m per year with an excellent track record of success.

Assessment: Some of the previous objectives were a little wordy. This one is positively verbose. It essentially says the job seeker wants a sales job and has some sales experience. The last line regarding quotas is good, although like the rest of the objective, it's a little wordy. Sales professionals are expected to work with a quota in most organizations. A sales professional should be able to tell what their past quotas were, and how their performance measured up to them.

Improvement: The first half of this is a waste. Almost all of it can be eliminated. In fact, we could cut just about everything except the goals of working in sales. Example: "Objective: Sales or Account Management role." Alternatively, we could keep some of the details, but tighten up the writing. Example: "Objective: Sales position using a consultative selling approach. Successful track record of exceeding quotas from $240k to $2m per year."

Chapter 8
Professional Summaries

A professional summary is an introductory section providing an overview of a job seeker's background along with a few key selling points. This is a teaser showing why you should be hired. It is designed to get the reader excited about reading your resume and motivate them to want to want to interview you.

Many resumes omit a summary section. They typically start with the education or work experience section of the resume. This is a mistake. In virtually every media, the standard is to provide a short introduction before moving into the detailed content. In movies, you see this with trailers and credits at the start of the movie, often followed by a high-energy action sequence to get things started. In books, there are almost always introductions and forwards, with some editions having three or four sections introducing the book. Newspapers and magazines always have titles, and often subtitles, for articles. They may even have a few sentences summarizing the article at the start.

In all of these different media, the authors or producers recognize that they need to capture the attention of the audience. This is critical to their success. Your resume is no different. It needs to have an introduction, and your name and address are not sufficient.

A professional summary gives you the ability to pack all of your best attributes into one section, and make this the first thing a hiring manager will read. It is your sales pitch - your reason why you should be interviewed and hired. An effective professional summary can improve the overall effectiveness of your resume.

You have a lot of flexibility in designing your professional summary. You can provide a broad overview of your background, list key skills, provide a description of key accomplishments, or brand yourself an expert in a particular field. The focus you choose is dependent upon the impression you want to make. Most job seekers will include a combination of these elements. The goal is to present the strongest presentation of your potential, and do it as briefly as possible.

There are a few elements you will want to include in your summary. These provide the most significant attributes you bring to the table. Although you don't need all of these, you should consider each and determine if it will improve your professional summary:

Progression: Provide a summary of your experience level and career progression

Skills: Show your skill level with key skills for the position. Key skills are the skills that are absolute non-negotiable requirements for the position. Focus on your most significant skills that are also the skills most in demand.

Accomplishments: Show one or more specific accomplishments where you delivered value to an employer. Typically, this will be in the form of revenue generation, cost savings, quality improvements, or customer service improvements.

Education: Does your educational background include elements that are especially impressive or sought after by hiring managers? If so, include these elements.

Remember your goal is to demonstrate your value and potential. This cannot be said enough. Every element of your resume needs to support this goal. A company will only hire you if they think you will add more value than it will cost to employ you. Regardless of your role, you need to contribute. If you do not contribute to the company, they are better off without you. This is a harsh reality, but it is a fundamental element of every business. If the business does not create value and generate an income, it will not survive.

This goes for any entity, even non-profits. The term non-profit is misleading. It implies that the organization does not generate more money that it started with. Every non-profit needs to generate capital. If the organization does not generate sufficient income or donations to support its operations, it will close.

When hiring, companies and hiring managers look for individuals to help the company succeed. The exact measures of success will vary from company to company and job to job, but the need to succeed is present in every organization.

You need to demonstrate how you will help the organization succeed. This requires showing your potential and demonstrating that potential with your past experiences and accomplishments. Ultimately, this is your sales pitch. You should be hired because you will create more value for the company than other candidates.

Each career field will have different measures for adding value. Some are very quantifiable and directly related to the bottom-line performance of a company. For example, a sales professional will need to generate sales and grow revenues for the company. It's easy to see the value this individual would offer. For other positions, particularly in support roles, the value added comes from the way the individual helps the organization operate more effectively. For example, a top IT professional could improve the uptime, usability and reliability of the company's systems. This then enables others in the company to be more effective.

Regardless of your role, you need to demonstrate the value you offer. Many job seekers rely on their work experience section for their primary sales pitch. They include experiences, projects and accomplishments under each job and hope the reader of their resume will read them all. Unfortunately, many get skipped. When a hiring manager reads your resume, they do not read every word from top to bottom. They scan the resume and skip around looking for the most important information. Often, the reader will only read for 15 to 30 seconds before making a decision to discard the resume. Even if you are highly qualified for a position, if the hiring manager does not see how you are qualified, you are likely to be rejected.

A professional summary allows you to stack the deck in your favor. You can pull out the elements that are most significant, and place them at the very top of your resume. Then, when a hiring manager reads your resume, your best selling points appear first and are much more likely to be read.

Designing a professional summary starts with creating a brand or theme. You need to present a clear message about who and what you are. Many job seekers fail to create any cohesive brand. Their resume is a patchwork of differing experiences that don't fit together very well. In fact, some resumes are downright confusing. A hiring manager will not spend a lot of time figuring out your background and potential. Companies receive plenty of resumes every day. There is no need to waste time on a resume that doesn't make sense. It is easier and faster just to move on to the next resume.

Your professional summary will make sense of your background. It will provide the glue that ties everything together. This creates an overall brand in the mind of the hiring manager. When this brand matches the image of what the hiring manager is looking for, you will motivate the hiring manager to want to interview you.

So, what is a brand on a resume? It is the overall impression or theme for what you offer. Remember, it all comes back to the value you will provide – your potential benefit to the company. Determining the brand and the theme for a resume are often difficult decisions for job seekers, but they don't need to be. You need to look at the opportunity you are pursuing, assess the way the position adds value to the organization, and show how you will succeed in these areas. That's it. Do that, and your resume will be much stronger and more effective.

The best thing about a professional summary is how flexible it can be. There is no strict formula for how it must be constructed and what must be included. In contrast, your work experience section does have some rules. You need to present your jobs in reverse chronological order. Each job needs to list the job title, employer dates and details of the position. There are a few commonly accepted structures for this. All in all, the work experience section should look very similar from resume to resume. This consistency helps hiring managers quickly digest a person's work experience and makes it easier to compare candidates.

The professional summary is different. You can do whatever you want. What format do you want: paragraphs, bulleted lists or a combination? All three structures are acceptable. Do you want to include information about your most recent job? Do you want to focus on a key skill or highlight a major accomplishment? Do you want a very short, concise summary, or a longer more detailed summary? There are no right answers to these questions. You have complete flexibility. What is important is whether the professional summary supports and promotes the theme of your resume, and if it is effective at attracting the interest of a hiring manager.

One way to think of a professional summary is that it is a mini resume. It is a summary section after all. It should summarize your resume, and summarize the value you offer. If a hiring manager reads only your professional summary, would it get them excited about you. If not, start over. Your professional summary needs to create excitement and interest.

Writing a Professional Summary

Hopefully, you are motivated to create a professional summary on your resume. The next step is actually doing it. Although most job seekers struggle with resume writing in general, and professional summaries in particular, it doesn't need to be difficult. We are going to walk through the process of creating a professional summary. Then, in later chapters, we will look at each step in the process in detail, and then review lots of examples.

To get started, we are going to create a professional summary in a format I really like. This format has three elements: a title, a branding statement, and a few bullet points. It is very easy to create, and easy to adapt as you customize your resume to different positions.

The first element is the title. This is the title of both your resume and the first section of the resume. We will look at choosing an effective title in detail in a later chapter. For now, we are going to use a job title representing the type of job being sought. This provides a good way to start to create a brand. It also takes care of providing an objective. For this exercise, we will consider an account manager experienced at selling a component used by other manufacturers to produce a product.

The title of the resume becomes "Account Manager."

The second element of the resume is the branding statement. This expands on the title and establishes the theme of the resume. An account manager could offer different benefits to an employer. The role can focus on new business development and prospecting, providing excellent customer service and retaining customers, or expanding sales with existing customers. The focus area will dictate the theme. For our account manager, we are going to focus on expanding sales with existing customers.

The branding statement becomes: "Successful sales professional with a track record of growing sales with established accounts and penetrating new departments and divisions. Highly skilled at obtaining referrals and leveraging referrals to land business. Consistently identifies opportunities within customers long before competitors, enabling significant influence on specifications ahead of the release of RFPs."

This branding statement is focused on how the account manager builds relationships with established customers, and leverages these relationships to grow sales. In some industries, there is a finite list of potential customers. Sales growth comes from expanding sales within these customers. In this example, the branding statement focuses on this type of sales, and reinforces the brand with statements related to specific aspects of the sales process.

The third element of the professional summary is a list of accomplishments. Every job seeker will claim to be exceptional, successful and very skilled in their field. This is to be expected. No one is going to say they are lousy and a poor performer. This means that every resume (or at least the vast majority of them) contain very positive statements about how great the job seeker is. Hiring managers will be very skeptical. They will not immediately believe that you are exceptional. You need to prove it to them.

The branding statement above is just a statement by the job seeker that they are great at sales. No matter how well written this branding statement is, it is ultimately just a claim by the job seeker. It is essentially the job seeker saying, "I'm really good at sales." To convince the hiring manager to believe this claim, the solution is straightforward. Prove to the hiring manager that you are as good as you claim.

To prove your claims, you need to show your past successes. Providing a few accomplishments demonstrating your contributions will make a great impression. You only need a few accomplishments, although more is usually better. In this example, we're going to add three accomplishments.

- **Account Penetration:** *Expanded a new account by identifying a wide range of applications for widgets at the customer, growing sales from $100k per quarter to more $800k per quarter over a two-year period.*
- **Open New Accounts:** *Used referrals within a company owned by a large conglomerate to open accounts in six other companies within the corporation, leading to $1.5 million in annual sales.*
- **Specification Adoption:** *Worked with engineers at a customer to design the specification for an $8 million*

widget project leading to the successful award of the contract.

These three bullets mirror the branding statement and provide specific, quantified results demonstrating past successes. They make the claims in the branding statement believable. They are also designed to pique the reader's interest. Ideally, the resume would be submitted to a hiring manager in an organization with a goal similar to one or more of these accomplishments.

Imagine a hiring manager whose primary goal for the year is to leverage an existing customer to break into other companies owned by the same corporation. Then, the hiring manager reads a resume with an accomplishment at the top where the job seeker did just that at another company. The hiring manager is going to be very interested and will take a closer look at this candidate.

Let's look at this professional summary in its entirety as it would appear on a resume:

Account Manager: *Successful sales professional with a track record of growing sales with established accounts and penetrating new departments and divisions. Highly skilled at obtaining referrals and leveraging referrals to land business. Consistently identifies opportunities within customers long before competitors, enabling significant influence on specifications ahead of the release of RFPs.*

- *Account Penetration:* *Expanded a new account by identifying a wide range of applications for widgets at the customer, growing sales from $100k per quarter to more $800k per quarter over a two-year period.*
- *Open New Accounts:* *Used referrals with a company owned by a large conglomerate to open accounts in six other companies within the corporation, leading to $1.5 million in annual sales.*
- *Specification Adoption:* *Worked with engineers at a customer to design the specification for an $8 million widget contract leading to the successful award of the contract.*

This professional summary will take up roughly a third of the first page of the resume. It creates a strong initial impression, and establishes a clear theme for the resume. This technique can be used by any job seeker for any position.

Chapter 9
Professional Summary Section Titles

When you write your professional summary, you should provide a title for the section. This isn't required, but it does offer a great way to get things started. The title of the section becomes the title of the resume. It offers a great way of branding the resume and establishing an initial theme.

As important as the title is, it is no wonder that some job seekers struggle with identifying the perfect title. They deliberate for days, trying to get it right, and second guess themselves every time they send out a resume. If this sounds like you, there is hope.

The first thing to remember is that there isn't a perfect title. You can't know what word or phrase will resonate the strongest with an individual hiring manager. You can only choose the title that will appeal to the majority of readers. Often, the best solution is keeping it simple by being direct. Your resume should not be a riddle that must be deciphered. It needs to convey information quickly; otherwise, you run the risk of the hiring manager moving on to the next candidate before they figure your resume out.

There are several types of titles you can choose for your resume. The easiest choice is to title the section "Professional Summary." This will work and many job seekers do this. The main drawback to this style is you miss a branding opportunity. The phrase professional summary does not convey any information about you.

The other types of titles include specific information about who you are. These typically take two forms: a job title or a keyword related to a skill. Either of these can be very effective.

If you choose a job title, you will establish a theme centered on that career. This is usually a good thing. You want to focus your resume on the job you are pursuing. The one exception to this is if you possess a skill that is in demand and is transferrable across a variety of jobs and industries. In this case, you might not want to pin yourself down to a single job. This is most likely a concern if you are posting your resume online. If you are applying for a specific position, you should focus your resume on that position as much as possible.

Choosing a keyword can also be effective. This can focus your brand even more than a job title if you use a keyword related to a specific aspect of a job. If you choose a keyword, make sure it relates to a skill that is in demand. Although a job may require a lot of skills, typically there is a very limited selection of these that a company struggles to find. If you possess one of these hard-to-find skills, your resume will quickly rise to the top of the pile. If you highlight a skill that is not in demand, you are unlikely to make a significant impression.

Typically, technical skills are better candidates for a resume title than non-technical skills. The technical skills that are in demand are constantly changing, and there is a limited candidate pool possessing these skills. Contrast this with soft skills such as communications or leadership skills. Everyone has communications skills. The skill levels vary widely from candidate to candidate, but everyone possesses an ability to communicate. Highlighting a soft skill is unlikely to grab a hiring manager's attention. It just doesn't differentiate the candidate enough. This is true even if the soft skill is one of the most critical skills of the position.

For example, consider a hiring manager who is looking for a project manager to lead a team of programmers. The most important skills the hiring manager is looking for are the ability to communicate effectively with the customer on projects and to deliver great customer service. These are soft skills, and every candidate is likely to claim they possess these skills.

Even though the soft skills are critically important, they are unlikely to be used during the initial screening of resumes. These are skills that are better assessed during the interview process, when the hiring manager can ask specific questions and observe the job seeker communicating the answers.

For the resume screening and assessment stage, the hiring manager is more likely to use technical skills for screening. These are easier to differentiate between candidates and allow the hiring manager to screen out a large number of unskilled candidates quickly. This serves the hiring manager's goals. A hiring manager needs to determine as quickly as possible which candidates should be interviewed. This requires rejecting as many candidates as possible to get to the top candidates. Any candidate who does not possess a required technical skill can be eliminated immediately without having to assess soft skills, a process that can take much more time to complete.

Often, a single technical skill will be in demand and used as the primary criterion even though a wide range of technical skills is required. In this case, the skill that is in demand is both rare and is likely to demonstrate proficiency in other skills. For example, consider a hiring manager looking for an administrative assistant who will use Outlook, Word and Excel on a regular basis. The hiring manager wants someone proficient with all three of these, but focuses on finding an expert with Excel. The reason for this is simple. Anyone who is an expert in Excel is likely to be proficient with Outlook and Word. Most computer users start by learning to send email, and then progress to writing text documents. Only after gaining this basic proficiency do they move on to spreadsheets. This makes Excel a good choice to screen for basic computer skills.

This same principle is used for setting requirements for a wide range of technical skills. Hiring managers will focus on the most difficult and rarest skills when initially screening resumes. When one of these skills is so critical to a job that it becomes the focal point of the search, the skill will make a great title for a resume.

Resume Title Examples

Virtually every job title and skill have been used at one time or another to start a resume. This does not mean they have all been effective. We are going to review a number of professional summary section titles and assess which are the best. Each of these is from an actual resume.

Senior Operations Professional

Assessment: This is overly generic. It could relate to almost any industry and a very wide range of career fields. Something a little more specific would be better.

IT Project Manager and Systems Engineer

Assessment: This is pretty good. It's a little longer than typical, but works well. The job seeker chooses to target two careers – project management and systems engineering. Because these two positions are directly related and within the same career field, they work well together. The candidate is essentially saying they want a project management role, but would consider working for a project manager as a systems engineer on a larger project. This is a lot to convey, and the title does it with six words.

Strategic Senior Telecom Professional / Executive

Assessment: This is a little wordy and not very specific. All we can deduce from this is that the job seeker wants a high level position in telecommunications. It could be shortened to "Senior Telecom Professional" or "Telecom Executive" without losing much. The word "strategic" is ok, but doesn't add a lot of value. Being strategic is important for telecom executives, but this is a soft skill that is unlikely to motivate a hiring manager.

Executive Management: Plant Manager Logistics

Assessment: This candidate needs to figure out where they fit in the organization. The executive management of a company is typically at a level above that of an operations manager in a manufacturing plant or distribution facility. This candidate is more likely looking for an operations role, either as a plant manager or logistics manager. Simplifying this and focusing on these two titles would be better. A good option would be to just list the two titles: "Plant Manager / Logistics Manager." Alternatively, the candidate could focus on executive level positions: "Manufacturing Operations Executive" or "Supply Chain Executive."

Senior Electrical Engineering Professional

Assessment: This is pretty good. It defines a specific career field — electrical engineering. The one thing that is missing is some clarification of what level the candidate is talking about. He could be referring to a senior design position, a management position or a senior management position. It isn't until halfway down the first page of the resume that the candidate explains that he has held VP of Engineering positions in the past. This confusion could easily be eliminated, and the candidate could establish a stronger initial brand by changing the word Professional to Leader or Manager.

Regional Vice President

Assessment: This is one of those cases where a job title doesn't tell enough of the story, but at the same time is too specific. The candidate leads a region of a financial services company, with a number of locations under him. Although the title is very specific, it doesn't capture the industry and role very well. A better option would be to focus on the core job functions. In this role, sales management is the primary responsibility. Focusing on this would be much better. For example, "Sales Management – Financial Services" better describes the candidate's background. Another option would be to focus on the executive level of the candidate. For example, "Financial Services Executive Leader" would capture both the industry and level of the job seeker.

Leadership Profile

Assessment: This example uses a section title similar to the phrase "Professional Summary," but focuses it on a single skill set. This technique can be effective, but leaves a lot of questions. Is this a front line supervisor or CEO? The title describes the section well. The candidate provides a detailed description of his leadership style. Unfortunately, this is unlikely to get a hiring manager excited. After reviewing the resume, the title makes even less sense. The candidate has an extensive engineering background and is looking to transition into engineer leadership. Despite starting the resume with a description of the candidate's leadership style, the resume is completely focused on the candidate's technical experience. There is nothing in the resume that conveys anything about leadership outside of the first section.

This is an example of resume that doesn't make sense. If the candidate truly wants a leadership position, where are the examples of the candidate's leadership experience and past successes? This confusion will discourage a hiring manager from considering the candidate for a leadership or a technical role. He doesn't have even the slightest leadership experience (at least according to his resume) and doesn't want a technical position. The candidate just killed his chances.

The candidate needs to change this. There are two options. First, he can focus the intro section on the technical skills and pursue a technical position. This is the easier option to implement. His resume is already focused on his technical skills. He would just have to rewrite the summary section to focus on those skills.

Second, he can focus on leadership experience and add examples of his leadership experience throughout his resume. Even if the candidate has never been in a management position, he will have had the opportunity to lead teams. The candidate can make a much stronger impression by demonstrating past leadership success by showing previous project and team leadership. Trying to demonstrate leadership ability by writing a few sentences on leadership style will do little to convince a hiring manager. For all we know, this job seeker copied a few sentences out of a book on leadership that he thought sounded good.

National Account Manager

Assessment: This is good. It's short and direct. The role of National Account Manager is very easy to understand.

President

Assessment: This title will not be effective. Although the title represents a specific position, it is a role that varies dramatically from company to company. More important than the role are the specific challenges the company is facing. A better title would focus on the industry and type of challenges. This candidate has worked in rapid growth high-tech companies and in turnaround situations. Either of these would make a good title. For example, "High-Tech Turnaround Specialist," "High-Tech Sales and Marketing Leader" or "IT Executive Leader." Each of these has a different perspective, and begins the process of creating a specific brand.

Merchandising Manager / Senior Buyer

Assessment: This is concise, direct and effective. The two job titles, Merchandising Manager and Senior Buyer, are directly related and go together well.

Management Professional

Assessment: Too vague. The term management designates a type of career, but the job seeker does not indicate what he is capable of managing. This individual is experienced in manufacturing management, and should indicate that in the title. Just because a person is a manager in one field does not mean they are qualified to lead in a completely different field. Would you take the General Manager of Major League Baseball team and put them in charge of a surgical center in a hospital? Both roles are management positions, but they are vastly different. Management and leadership are transferrable, but they are not the only skills needed to lead an organization. A much better title for this individual would be "Manufacturing Manager."

Chapter 10
Professional Summary Section Content

Your professional summary will include information on your experience, skills, accomplishments, education and other aspects of your background and abilities. It is a summary of your career, and needs to demonstrate your potential value to an employer. The scope of information that can be conveyed in a professional summary is extensive. It's a lot of ground to cover, and you need to be brief. Your professional summary is just a summary. It is designed to generate interest and impress the reader enough to want to learn more.

Fortunately, you are not trying to get hired based on the summary section alone. Your goal is to create an image of what you bring to the table. You want to pique the reader's interest and motivate them to want to learn more. A successful summary section will cause the hiring manager to want to read the rest of the resume closely. The ultimate goal of your resume is to motivate the hiring manager to want to interview you.

The key to an effective professional summary is including only the most important elements of your background. The judge of what is important is ultimately the hiring manager. A detail that is significant to you, but unimportant to a hiring manager should not be in your summary section (and probably should not be in your resume). Your resume is not written to impress you. It is a sales document, and needs to be designed to sell your potential to an employer.

Almost anything from your background can go in your professional summary. Prioritizing information is critical. Previously, we noted how you might include details of your progression, skills, accomplishments and education. This is just a starting point, but covers the most common elements to include. We will now look at each of these areas in detail.

Progression

You want to demonstrate that you have the experience and expertise to succeed in a position. Providing a summary of your experience is a good way to show this. Summarizing your experience can often be done with only a few words.

Example: "20+ years of manufacturing leadership experience"

This conveys an experience level that is easy to understand, and will be effective for many job seekers. Despite this, the summary does not provide a lot of detail. If your career progression is a major selling point, you may expand on this.

Example: "15 year progression from supervisor to VP of Manufacturing, with a track record of improving productivity."

This example not only conveys the years of experience, but it also talks about the promotions the job seeker received leading to the VP of Manufacturing role. It adds a claim about a track record of productivity improvements. This type of claim can be effective, but remember to add accomplishments demonstrating specific results.

Skills

Your skills are a critical element of your background. You need to demonstrate them to a hiring manager. Focus on the most significant skills to the hiring manager. These are the skills that are most important and difficult to find. You also want to lead with your strength. Don't put a skill at the top of your resume just because it is a popular skill. Put it there because you are truly accomplished with the skill.

Each industry and career field will have a different set of skills that are important. You will need to research your industry to determine the most significant and most in demand skills. You probably already have a good idea of what to prioritize. We will look at a few examples for a selection of careers.

Manufacturing: Lean Manufacturing and Six Sigma have been hot topics. These can make good skills to highlight, along with other continuous improvement skills.

Example: "Accomplished lean manufacturing expert, experienced at implementing lean methodologies to cut lead times, reduce inventory levels and improve productivity."

Sales: In sales careers, the primary skills required are related to sales activities. As basic as this is, focusing on these skills is absolutely essential. Sales is a career field where each individual needs to demonstrate their personal success. Highlighting sales skills, particularly skills related to cold calling, prospecting, new business development and opening new accounts can be an important differentiator for a job seeker.

Example: "Hunter/rainmaker, highly skilled at prospecting and opening new accounts."

IT: In IT, technical skills are often the most important element when assessing job seekers. For the most sought after skills, a candidate can bring almost any background as long as they possess the skill.

Example: "Expert programmer with AJAX, VB.net, Ruby and Ruby on Rails"

Accomplishments

No matter how much experience you have and what skills you claim to possess, if you have never been successful, you will have a hard time impressing a hiring manager. Companies do not hire resumes, and they don't want any warm body that will just show up. They need people to perform specific tasks at a high performance level. You need to show you can perform at a high level. Even more important, you need to show how you will add more value than your competition.

The most effective way to show the value you will provide is to present the value you have provided in the past. To do this, list several accomplishments where you delivered a quantified result. The key to presenting accomplishments is to be specific. You must show what you did and what your results were.

Accomplishments that are too general will not make a positive impression. They will be forgotten as quickly as they are read, and they will discourage the reader from reading more. For example, I read a resume from a job seeker who claimed he had delivered $100 million in cost savings. This is a big number, and might sound good at first, but it doesn't tell us anything. The accomplishment was placed in the professional summary section and likely was a career total, including every dollar the job seeker had been involved in saving over his career. We can't tell what the job seeker did to save that money.

A much better approach is to be specific. Provide a clear explanation of what you did and what the results were. Below are a couple of accomplishments for manufacturing professional.

- **Implemented Lean:** *Led a Lean Implementation as the manufacturing manager of a Tier 1 automotive supplier with responsibility for over 800 production workers and supervisors. Completed the implementation over a two-year period, resulting in a 60% reduction in lead times and a 25% improvement in productivity.*
- **Reduced Scrap:** *Improved yields on a production line, reducing scrap from 5% to less than 1%, saving $185,000 per year.*

In both cases, it is clear what the job seeker accomplished. Examples of past successes like these will make a very strong impression on a resume.

Education

Your educational background may be highly valued by an employer. Candidates with advanced degrees that are in demand should emphasize their education. Other job seekers possessing valued certifications or who completed continuing education classes can highlight those. Just remember to focus on what is valued by an employer. Usually, you should only list degrees and certifications in the professional summary. Classes without any qualification of what was learned are not nearly as impressive. Anyone can show up to a seminar, and showing up doesn't mean a person learned anything they will apply in their career.

Examples: "Ph.D. in Computer Science," "CFA – Charted Financial Analyst," or "LEED-AP BD+C: LEED Accredited Professional in Building Design and Construction."

Chapter 11
Professional Summary Organization

There is a wide range of styles and structures for a professional summary section. Just as the content can be adapted, so can the organization. Some job seekers choose to write with short paragraphs. Others use long blocks of text. Still others use bulleted lists. Although the choice of format is a personal style choice, the design and organization of the professional summary will make it more or less effective.

When writing a professional summary, you should use short blocks of text. We live in a world where a large segment of the population is conditioned to read and write in 140 character blocks. Many of the hiring managers who will read your resume will be more comfortable with short paragraphs. Long paragraphs are unlikely to be read. If they are read, it is likely only the first line or two will be read.

A better technique is to break blocks of text into short paragraphs. This will make your resume appear easier to read, and increase the amount of your resume that is read.

Where possible, you should also use bullet points. Readers are drawn to bulleted lists. Many people subconsciously assume that the bulleted information will be more important than the information in paragraph form. Any time you can add a bulleted list, you improve the odds of the reader focusing on that content.

Your professional summary needs to be a summary. This may sound obvious, but surprisingly, there are job seekers who don't get it. There are resumes where the professional summary takes up more than half the resume. When your summary is longer than the content you are summarizing, there is something wrong. A good rule of thumb is to keep the summary to 10% to 20% of the resume. For an average resume with 750 words, that means the summary should be 75 to 150 words. This isn't a hard and fast rule, but is a good guide for an effective range.

Some job seekers include keyword lists in their professional summary. Some even give these lists a title, such as core competencies or skills. The lists do a good job of presenting a number of skills in a little space, but they aren't very effective at the top of a resume. You can list any skills you want on your resume, but you are unlikely to impress a hiring manager with just a list of words. Anyone can put a list of keywords at the top of their resume. The list will not convey your skill level, experience and accomplishments with the skills. To impress a hiring manager, you need to demonstrate how you will add value using the skills.

Let's look at a few examples of structures. We are not going to get into formatting techniques. The examples will include some minimum formatting, but do not provide all the formatting options. There is a wide range of format choices, including fonts, font sizes, indenting, alignment, text formatting and other techniques. Our focus is on the structure and organization of the information.

We are going to use a production manager seeking a manufacturing leadership position as the candidate. Each example will illustrate a different structure. After each example, an assessment of the effectiveness of the structure is provided. When reviewing these, notice how the choice of structure has a significant effect on the type of content incorporated in the summary.

Example 1: A title followed by a paragraph

> *Professional Summary*
> *Production Manager with 15 years of experience in automotive and textile industries. Demonstrated exceptional leadership, motivational and communication skills, high mechanical aptitude, strong problem solving skills, excellent process management, and good cost reduction initiative. Specific skills include Lean Manufacturing, Six Sigma, production scheduling, MRP systems, inventory control, project management, proficiency in Microsoft Word and Excel, computer controlled manufacturing and robotics equipment, and various textile and paper printing presses. Highly motivated and results-oriented with the demonstrated ability to drive performance and maximize productivity.*

This example has a fairly large block of text and lists a wide range of skills. Did you read the entire paragraph, or skip ahead midway through? Would you read the entire paragraph if you had 200 resumes in your inbox that you need to screen? The summary has a lot of great keywords, but does little to demonstrate the skill level the job seeker possesses. It also fails to include any accomplishments. The title of the section is placed on the line above the paragraph and uses the general title professional summary. Overall, this is typical of many professional summaries, but is far from ideal. It won't hurt the candidate's chances, but doesn't do a lot to sell the candidate's potential.

Example 2: A title and paragraph together

> ***Production Manager:*** *Automotive and textile manufacturing leader with 15 years of experience. Demonstrated exceptional leadership, motivational and communication skills, high mechanical aptitude, strong problem solving skills, excellent process management, and good cost reduction initiative. Specific skills include Lean Manufacturing, Six Sigma, production scheduling, MRP systems, inventory control, project management, proficiency in Microsoft Word and Excel, computer controlled manufacturing and robotics equipment, and various textile and paper printing presses. Highly motivated and results-oriented with the demonstrated ability to drive performance and maximize productivity.*

In this example, the job title is presented at the start of the paragraph. This can be an effective way to draw the reader into the paragraph. When the title is presented above the paragraph, some readers may read the title and skip past the summary, especially if it is a lengthy paragraph. Putting the title inside the paragraph won't ensure the summary is read, but it should improve the odds. The remainder of the summary is identical to the first example, and will have limited effectiveness.

Example 3: A title and a short paragraph followed by a keyword list

> ***Production Manager:*** *Successful manufacturing leader with 15 years of experience within the automotive and textile industries. Consistently cut costs, reduced lead times, cut inventories and improved quality.*
>
> *Lean Manufacturing * Kanban * Production Scheduling * Inventory Control * MRP Systems * Project Management * 5S * MRP Systems * Budget Forecasting * JIT * Quality Assurance * TQM * ISO 9000/1 * Process Mapping * Value Stream Mapping * Root Cause Analysis * MS Project*

This example is typical of many resumes. It starts with a title and a branding statement, and then provides a keyword list. Keyword lists can range from short lists with a just a few keywords to lists with more than fifty terms. Throwing a bunch of keywords on the top of a resume will not get a hiring manager excited. Even worse, many job seekers use acronyms in their keyword lists. One resume I read contained a list of 19 three-letter acronyms in the summary section. It's hard to imagine this presentation impressing anyone.

The only time a keyword will attract attention is when the skill is in incredible demand. There are IT skills that are so hard to find that anyone that claims to even know about one of these technologies will get an interview. Skills like this may only have a handful of people in the world that know the technology. Typically, this level of demand only last a short time, perhaps a few months. Then, more people get trained and learn the technology and demand drops. It is unlikely there will be other situations where a person can put a couple of words at the top of the resume, and that will generate a lot of interest.

The length of the keyword list is also an issue. When adding more than a few keywords, the large number of terms only serves to dilute the impact of each keyword. It is likely you possess hundreds of skills, but putting them all on your resume at the top is a mistake. You need to choose a primary area of focus, and create a sales pitch emphasizing the skills in that area.

Example 4: Multiple Titles and a paragraph

Project Management ~ Supply Chain Management ~ Operations Management

Automotive and textile manufacturing leader with 15 years of experience. Demonstrated exceptional leadership, motivational and communication skills, high mechanical aptitude, strong problem solving skills, excellent process management, and good cost reduction initiative. Specific skills include Lean Manufacturing, Six Sigma, production scheduling, MRP systems, inventory control, project management, proficiency in Microsoft Word and Excel, computer controlled manufacturing and robotics equipment, and various textile and paper printing presses. Highly motivated and results-oriented with the demonstrated ability to drive performance and maximize productivity.

This example provides a short keyword list as the title of the resume. With this format, the list usually has three phrases. When job seekers use this structure, they are often trying to cover all their bases. They want to pursue multiple career paths, and don't want to limit their resume to just one. Their solution: list all three. This technique only serves to confuse the reader. Your resume is a sales pitch designed to lead to an interview. Each time you submit your resume, you are applying for a single job – not every conceivable job you may be qualified for. You need to focus on that one job, and develop the strongest sales pitch for it.

The problem is a little more difficult when you post your resume online. You need to choose an area of focus even if you have multiple goals. There isn't an easy answer to this. The more you focus your presentation, the more effective your resume will be, but the fewer number of opportunities that will fall in your area of focus.

In a previous chapter, we looked at a job seeker who used two job titles as the title of the resume. In that case, the job titles were within the same career field. One of the positions was a direct supervisor for the other position. This will not be confusing to a hiring manager. It is understandable that a job seeker may consider a job at one level but prefer the position one level up from it. Often, when moving from a smaller to a larger company, you will have to take a slightly lower position. The reverse is also true. It is often easier to move to a higher level when moving into a smaller organization.

In this summary example, the candidate is trying to carve out three career fields: project management, supply chain management and operations management. Although related, they are distinct. The candidate will be better off to choose one area for each version of his resume.

Example 5: Title, multiple keywords and a paragraph

Production Manager

Lean Manufacturing ~ Six Sigma ~ Leadership

Automotive and textile manufacturing leader with 15 years of experience. Demonstrated exceptional leadership, motivational and communication skills, high mechanical aptitude, strong problem solving skills, excellent process management, and good cost reduction initiative. Specific skills include Lean Manufacturing, Six Sigma, production scheduling, MRP systems, inventory control, project management, proficiency in Microsoft Word and Excel, computer controlled manufacturing and robotics equipment, and various textile and paper printing presses. Highly motivated and results-oriented with the demonstrated ability to drive performance and maximize productivity.

This example includes the technique of using a short three-word list as a title but makes some significant improvements over example 4. First, the resume has a main title – Production Manager. This provides an overall focus for the resume. Second, the list of words is not a list of job titles, but a list of skills. The job seeker uses the list to further focus the resume. The candidate isn't just a production manager. They are a production manager who is an expert in lean manufacturing, Kanban and turnarounds. Well, actually, we don't know it the candidate is an expert in these areas – they are just words thrown at the top of the resume. It is a branding statement designed to convey a level of expertise, but by itself does not provide any proof of the job seeker's expertise level.

The example continues with a paragraph describing the candidate's background and skills. The paragraph reinforces the theme of the title and keywords, but it doesn't provide any qualification of the candidate's skill. There is nothing, other than the statement of 15+ years of experience, that shows how good the candidate is with these skills or whether he has been successful as a production manager in the past. Adding some accomplishments would improve this.

Example 6: The bulleted list

Career Highlights

- 10+ years of experience leading manufacturing operations
- CPIM – Certified in Production and Inventory Management by APICS
- Implemented Lean: Led a Lean Implementation as the manufacturing manager of a Tier 1 automotive supplier with responsibility for over 800 production workers and supervisors. Completed the implementation over a two-year period, resulting in a 60% reduction in lead times and a 25% improvement in productivity.
- Reduced Scrap: Improved yields on a production line, reducing scrap from 5% to less than 1%, saving $185,000 per year.

This bulleted list provides highlights from the job seeker's background and can draw attention to the most significant elements. This is an improvement over most summary sections, but it is still far from perfect. One goal of an introductory section is to introduce the resume. By omitting a title or branding statement, the format misses the opportunity to create an initial impression.

Example 7: Title and paragraph followed by accomplishments

Production Manager: *Automotive and textile manufacturing leader with 15 years of experience. Consistently cut costs, reduced lead times, cut inventories and improved quality.*

- *Implemented Lean: Led a Lean Implementation as the manufacturing manager of a Tier 1 automotive supplier with responsibility for over 800 production workers and supervisors. Completed the implementation over a two-year period, resulting in a 60% reduction in lead times and a 25% improvement in productivity.*
- *Reduced Scrap: Improved yields on a production line, reducing scrap from 5% to less than 1%, saving $185,000 per year.*

This example provides a great format to start a resume. It has a title that clearly establishes the career field of the candidate. The title is followed by two short sentences that provide an overview of the job seeker. With the title and paragraph, the resume's theme is established. There are claims made about past successes, and these need to be backed up with accomplishments. The two bullets do just that. They provide specific examples of contributions made by the candidate.

Each bullet point includes a bolded title. This is a great technique for drawing attention to your most significant and important accomplishments. Remember, the importance of something in your resume is determined by the reader, not you. Your resume needs to impress hiring managers. Each hiring manager will be looking for a different set of skills, experiences and accomplishments, and will focus on the elements of your resume that most closely match this. By providing a title for accomplishments, you can draw attention to the accomplishments that relate most closely to the challenges the hiring manager faces. For example, picture a VP of Manufacturing that needs to hire a production manager. The plant is running well but has a scrap problem. Reducing scrap will be the most significant objective of the production manager during the first year on the job. The title "Reduced Scrap" will jump off the page and grab this VP's attention. It will talk directly to the primary goal and biggest need for the position.

You can't know what the top issues a hiring manager is trying to address when filling a position. Job descriptions are typically too vague to determine what the hot issues are for the position. Because of this, you need to list multiple accomplishments addressing different aspects of the job. Some or all of these should make a strong impression with the hiring manager.

The example provides two accomplishments. If this is all you have, that's ok. It is a much stronger presentation than the examples without accomplishments. Ideally, you will have more than two accomplishments to highlight. At a minimum, try to list at least 3 to 5 accomplishments. The more the better. Past accomplishments are usually the most impressive part of a resume. Just remember that your professional summary is a summary. It should not be much longer than half of a page (a quarter of the resume). If you have more accomplishments you want to include, put them in your work experience section. That section should be packed with accomplishments, and each job you have held should list at least a couple of successes.

Choosing a Style

We just looked at 7 styles of professional summaries, and assessed the strengths and weaknesses of each. This is far from an exhaustive list. There are numerous variations on these. In some cases, the structure is important. In others, it is just a stylistic choose. More often, the choice of content is the most critical decision. You can have the best formatted summary section, but if the text is vague, poorly written and devoid of any substance, you will not make a good impression.

Try some of the styles. Just remember a few of the recommendations from the examples:

1. Focus your resume on the job you are pursuing. Do not try to be all things to all employers.
2. Be concise. Using fewer words is better. You want to convey your brand and value proposition as quickly as possible and encourage the hiring manager to keep reading.
3. Incorporate accomplishments. Your past successes will do more to sell a hiring manager on your potential than anything else will.
4. Avoid the keyword dump. Listing numerous keywords at the top of your resume will not impress anyone. If something is important enough to be placed at the top of your resume, make sure you explain it.
5. Add titles to your bullet points. Titles are a great way to summarize a bullet point and highlight something in it. This also allows the reader to scan the titles and quickly choose the ones that are most interesting and impressive.

Chapter 12
Professional Summary Examples

In the previous chapter, we looked at seven styles of professional summaries. All the examples were for the same hypothetical candidate, and demonstrate how to present the information in the professional summary. It is now time to look as some actual professional summary sections.

Each professional summary listed is from an actual job seeker, with only minor changes to the text in order to ensure the anonymity of the job seeker. These show a wide range of styles and content. After each example, an assessment is provided.

The examples are presented without a lot of formatting. Typically, these would be formatted using different alignments, fonts, font sizes and other techniques. It is important to create as professional a presentation as possible, but for our purposes, we want to focus on the content and organization. Later, we will address formatting.

Reviewing these examples is one of the best ways to learn how to write an effective professional summary. When you work on your resume, you are only looking at one resume. What may look good and make sense to you may be completely confusing and ineffective to a hiring manager trying to screen 100 resumes. Look at the examples as if you are a hiring manager considering the candidate. This will teach you to assess your resume better, and ultimately help you produce a better, more effective resume.

Example 1: Advertising/Public Relations Professional

Professional Summary

Dedicated professional with 15+ years of experience in Advertising, Public Relations and Merchandising.

Summary of qualifications

- *Excellent skill at developing communications programs*

- *Outstanding creative and graphic design abilities*

- *Team oriented with a proven track record of success*

- *Solid corporate event/tradeshow experience*

- *Computer proficient with all versions of Photoshop, Indesign, Illustrator, Microsoft Word and Excel*

Assessment: The summary provides an overview of the skills of the job seeker and provides a clear brand. The brand isn't very enticing, though. There is nothing indicating the job seeker's skill level or past success. The skills listed are good and essential for this career field, but many are skills everyone in the field would be expected to have. It's difficult to imagine someone developing marketing materials today without experience with Photoshop. Because of this, the resume is likely to look like every other resume in the pile. There is little to nothing to indicate that the job seeker is exceptional in any way.

The job seeker would do better to include some qualification of the type and scope of work and provide quantified results. For example, the bullet discussing trade show experience provides nothing detailing this experience. It doesn't indicate if the job seeker designed trade show displays, managed trade show attendance, or organized trade shows. A much better tactic would be to provide a couple of examples of the experience. For example:

> *Led tradeshow strategy and management, including booth design, event selection and event management for more than 20 tradeshows per year, generating more than 15,000 leads and $5 million in revenues.*

This bullet provides a clear description of what the job seeker did with tradeshows and is far more impressive than the original bullet. Most importantly, the bullet lists specific results that are likely to attract attention and impress hiring managers.

The candidate is actually an advertising manager at a large manufacturing company, with an excellent set of experiences. Unfortunately, the professional summary creates an impression of a low-level graphic designer. Nothing in this summary creates an image of a corporate manager directing the advertising, marketing and communications strategy for a corporation. This summary section will hurt the job seeker's chances. There is a good chance the candidate could be rejected based on the summary alone.

It is especially surprising that an advertising manager created this resume. Using generic titles, such as Professional Summary and Summary of Qualifications, misses a great branding opportunity. There is nothing in this example that indicates an ability to create a great ad or marketing plan. This is unfortunate because the job seeker is likely to be judged on the presentation of the resume as an indication of advertising skill. This is a common mistake. Many job seekers focus on creating what they think is a professional presentation, but in fact, they create an unimpressive, sterile and ineffective resume.

Example 2: Operations Management/Business Development Executive

OPERATIONS MANAGEMENT • BUSINESS DEVELOPMENT

PROFESSIONAL SUMMARY:

Business Executive with more than 20 years of progressive sales, marketing and management experience, in the healthcare and insurance fields, leading to executive level leadership and operations management affecting bottom line results. A change agent who combines leadership, sales and marketing skills, P&L accountability and strategic planning abilities to deliver business process improvement. Excels at leveraging key relationships and coaching employees to develop and add value across the organization. Executive level leadership with a extensive administration, planning and oversight experience. Committed to delivering the highest levels of customer service and quality.

Background includes consulting experience in the areas or risk management, policy analysis, claims disputes and market strategy.

SALES/MARKETING

Extensive experience leading sales efforts to build the customer base, grow revenues and improve profit margins.

- *Researched and analyzed industry trends, competition and customer demographic changes to identify opportunities to gain competitive advantages and leverage these opportunities.*

- *Developed and implemented innovative marketing strategies utilizing a wide range of advertising media to build customer awareness.*
- *Excellent communication and interpersonal skills.*

MANAGEMENT

Extensive background leading operations and personnel, including executive profit & loss responsibility.

- *Administered budgets, analyzed performance and identified opportunities to reduce costs.*
- *Developed and implemented strategic plans and objectives.*
- *Monitored internal controls and identified weaknesses. Developed and implemented strategies to effectively improve policies and procedures.*
- *Led the development of staffing plans and oversaw the recruitment, selection, training, development and evaluation of personnel.*
- *Substantial leadership, decision-making and supervisory experience, as well as extensive conflict resolution skills.*

Assessment: This is a very long summary section. At 259 words, it takes up more than a third of the entire resume. Did you read the entire summary section, or skip to the assessment? Because of the length, the summary is presented in three sections. First, there is an overall summary, and then the candidate presents details of his sales/marketing and management background.

The summary is way too long and has very little valuable content. It starts with two keyword phrases representing different career fields. The job seeker needs to pick a career field. This confusion continues throughout the summary with the job seeker presenting a section for each field.

Apart from the structure and multiple career fields, the section has other problems. The first sentence is 32 words long. This is way too long, and is likely to cause the reader to skip the rest of the summary section. It would be much better to break this up into several sentences. The first sentence should end after "management experience" or "insurance fields." This shorter sentence would provide a better start to the section.

Despite being extremely long, the summary section offers very little value. The bulk of the content lists past responsibilities the job seeker has held. Being responsible for something does not mean you were good at it. Listing nothing but responsibilities creates an impression of a seat warmer. Did this candidate successfully show up and keep the seat warm throughout his career, or did he do something while he was there? I'm sure the candidate had some great successes over his career, but a hiring manager screening hundreds of resumes is not going to assume you did anything you don't tell them. If it isn't on your resume, it didn't happen. Hiring managers look for past successes. If you don't present any, then you weren't successful. That is not the impression this candidate, or any other candidate, wants to make.

A better option would be to shorten this down dramatically, focus on one career field and add several accomplishments.

Example 3: CFO

Chief Financial Officer

* Finance * Treasury * Operations *Manufacturing *
Information Systems

Highly experienced financial and operations executive with
international experience in accounting, financial reporting,
manufacturing, logistics, distribution, strategic planning,
start up and growth corporations, IT, and human resources.
A proven track record for increasing the bottom line
performance. Entrepreneurial self-starter with a "roll-up
your sleeves," get it done attitude.

Selected Achievements

- *Spearheaded major restructuring initiatives resulting*
  in improvements in the overall expense structure.
- *Negotiated and secured all funding, including multi-*
  million dollar asset based credit lines.
- *Realized annual savings of over $1.5 million dollars*
  by identifying alternative capital sources and
  implementing additional financing arrangements.
- *Successfully led a corporation through a leveraged*
  buyout with a leading private equity firm.
- *Increased bottom line profitability by $1 million*
  annually by developing and implementing a regional
  corporate office strategy in foreign markets.
- *Selected and administered the company's health and*
  business insurance plans, saving the company over
  35% per year in related costs.

- *Selected and implemented Accounting and ERP systems.*

Core Competencies:

Accounting/Finance ~ Cost Accounting ~ Strategic Planning ~ Manufacturing/Distribution ~ Operations Management ~ IT System Implementation ~ HR/Benefits ~ International Operations ~ Business Expansion & Startups

Assessment: This summary is pretty long, more than 200 words. It has some great content, and overall is pretty good. The section starts with a job title "Chief Financial Officer." This provides a clear indication of what the job seeker is looking for and an idea of the background of the job seeker. The next line provides five keyword phrases. The keywords are general and unrelated. As a result, this line doesn't add much value. It would be better at this stage to stay focused and establish a clear theme.

The paragraph describing the job seeker's background is very broad and covers a wide range of disciplines. Ordinarily, this would be a big mistake. In this case, the individual is looking for a senior executive role where a breadth of experiences is valuable. For roles like this, there needs to be a balance of providing a specific focus and demonstrating versatility. A CFO will affect every aspect of the company, and needs to have at least some familiarity of the challenges, issues and performance drivers for every discipline. The paragraph covers this breadth but doesn't provide enough focus to go with it. What is missing is a clear theme. The paragraph ends up being an unimpressive list of unrelated stuff. A better approach will focus on a clear theme. Consider this rewrite of the paragraph:

Successful financial executive skilled in international logistics operations. Entrepreneurial self-started, with a "roll-up your sleeves," get it done attitude able to provide strategic and financial guidance to all aspects of a logistics operation. Skilled at establishing financing for rapidly changing organizations, including startups and high-growth ventures.

This rewrite provides a definite theme. It focuses on one industry and a specific type of role. Although CFO positions have a lot of similarities, they can vary greatly from company to company due to the specific challenges faced by each corporation.

After the summary paragraph, the job seeker lists several accomplishments. These are great. Any time you can demonstrate your past success, you will make a better impression. The accomplishments touch on a range of activities. This breadth is good. You can't know what the exact needs of a company are going to be, and should provide examples of past successes in multiple areas.

Note that some of the accomplishments do not have specific measurable results. The best accomplishments will be clear, concise and have specific numbers attached. Despite this, not all of your successes will have a quantified result. The job seeker does a good job of mixing together accomplishments with numeric results with the accomplishments that don't. The presentation is effective.

The section concludes with a keyword dump. This is a waste of space. The summary section would be more effective if this was deleted.

Overall, the inclusion of specific accomplishments makes this is a pretty good summary section, and it is likely to be effective. With a few small changes, it could be a real winner.

Example 4: Unknown Career Field

OBJECTIVE: To secure a position utilizing my skills and past experiences to succeed in new challenges with opportunities for growth.

SUMMARY OF QUALIFICATIONS:

- *Proven ability to understand and follow complex instructions to successful conclusions*
- *Dynamic leader and team builder, consistently motivating others toward success.*
- *Strong problem solving, analytical, organizational, and communication skills*

Assessment: This job seeker decided to start with an objective statement and follow it with a summary section. This is not unusual. Unfortunately, it's not particularly effective either. The objective statement doesn't say anything. It is a complete waste of space. Even worse, it is the first thing on the resume, so the job seeker leads off by making an impression of wasting the reader's time... not a good start.

The qualifications section provides a list of soft skills. Although these skills are extremely important to almost any career, their presentation will do little to impress a hiring manager. There's just nothing of substance here.

What is this job seeker's career field? Is there anything in the summary section that allows you to make a guess? You might conclude that this person could be in a supervisory role, but that is about it. The candidate is actually an engineering manager from a high tech company. Unfortunately, there is nothing in the summary that conveys anything about engineering, design, or technology. This person needs to be a source of leadership for creativity, innovation and design, but never mentions anything related to these attributes.

The summary also fails to demonstrate any past successes. As with other careers, listing accomplishments is essential.

Example 5: Business Development

MANAGER: NEW BUSINESS DEVELOPMENT / SALES

TOP-PRODUCING MANAGEMENT PROFESSIONAL with extensive experience leading operations, sales and marketing initiatives for the technology industry with a proven track record of revenue growth. Passionate about team building and management through mentoring and education. Rainmaker with an ability to identify customer needs, position products and services for market growth, and exceed customer expectations. Highly effective leveraging strategic relationships and negotiation / presentation skills to surpass sales targets.

LEADERSHIP SKILLS

- *Business Development Management*
- *Market Penetration / Sales Growth Strategies*
- *Negotiation / Presentation Skills*
- *Team Leadership & Performance Management*
- *Mentoring and Professional Development*
- *Product / Solution Selling Approaches*
- *Competitive Product Positioning*

Assessment: The summary section does a good job of establishing a clear theme. Resumes from sales professionals typically do a much better job at conveying a focused value proposition than resumes from other fields. This is to be expected. Sales professionals are taught to focus on the value they offer a prospect.

Usually, they are focused on a product or service, but it is easy to apply this skill to their resumes.

The summary creates the theme in the first sentence, and then expands on this theme throughout the paragraph. It sounds really good and touches on some of the details hiring managers look for. For example, the job seeker describes himself as a rainmaker. This is a term for a person who can go out on their own and generate new sales from new customers in a new industry. True rainmakers can be some of the most valuable people in a company. They are very rare and sought after. The rainmaker quality directly supports the overall theme of the summary section, as do the other qualities mentioned in the section.

Although the rainmaker claim is a good one for a sales position, this candidate is pursuing a management position. The emphasis of the summary is on individual sales performance, but the targeted role requires driving success through a team. This is likely to create an impression with a hiring manager that the candidate is better suited for a sales position and not a management position.

In addition, the job seeker fails to show any successes. This summary would be much more effective if there were a few examples of the job seeker growing sales directly, or building a team that increased revenues.

The last piece of the summary is a list of keyword phrases. This adds little to no value. The resume would be more effective without this list.

Example 6: Sales Professional #1

Areas of Competency: Professional Sales

Profile

A self motivated professional with a good knowledge of sales and marketing theories, along with strong business experience. I am friendly, enthusiastic and persuasive in sales situations and able to build excellent rapport and strong customer relationships with prospects of all socio-economic backgrounds. I fully understand the commitment required to exceed customer expectations and possess the organizational skills and determination to surpass all sales goals. I possess excellent skills in the development of sales and marketing plans and promotional materials, and am accomplished delivering very persuasive and effective sales presentations. Computer skills: Word, Excel, and Powerpoint.

Assessment: The summary section starts with the line "Areas of Competency: Professional Sales." Although the job seeker uses the plural "Areas," he only lists one competency. This start to the section is weak and uninspiring. He would be better off with a simple title "Sales Professional." Adding a title like this would also eliminate the need for the title "Profile" on the next line.

The summary paragraph the job seeker wrote is as uninspiring as the title. The first line focuses on his knowledge of sales and marketing theories. This will turn off most sales managers. A sales manager couldn't care less about a sales rep's knowledge of sales theories. What matters is whether the job seeker can sell. Reading the entire paragraph, the sales rep never states that he is good at selling. Can he prospect and open new accounts? Is he a good closer? Does he know how to increase sales to existing customers? We don't know because the candidate doesn't tell us.

A much better summary would focus on results. Sales is a field where numbers are usually readily available. It is tough to find a successful sales professional who doesn't know how much they sold (and how much they earned in commissions). This job seeker has the stats to establish a track record of success. Buried in the work experience section are numerous examples where the job seeker had delivered substantial sales growth, beat quotas and earned sales awards from employers. To maximize the effectiveness of the resume, these accomplishments need to be in the professional summary.

Example 7: Sales Professional #2

CAREER SUMMARY

Highly successful sales executive with a solid record of delivering sales growth, profitability and customer loyalty in a B2B manufacturing environment. Adept at penetrating and establishing relationships with Fortune 1000 companies and presenting to all levels of corporate structure. Loyal, personable, hard working individual with more 20 years of sales experience. An enthusiastic team player not afraid to get his hands dirty.

Core Competencies

- *Relationship Building*
- *Interpersonal Understanding*
- *Strategic Planning*
- *Problem Solver*
- *Organizational Awareness*
- *Team Player*

Assessment: This example is only marginally better than the previous example. The big difference is the job seeker starts the summary with a strong statement of past sales success. This creates the right initial impression. The rest of the summary is a description of the job seeker that focuses on style, personality and soft skills. Although there is nothing bad about the description, there is little to get a hiring manager excited. Looking at this from a classic sales approach, the job seeker presents many features with no benefits to the customer. Customers buy benefits not features, and this summary section has few benefits.

The choice of items in the bulleted list is also ineffective. The skills presented aren't bad. They may be valuable. It's just very difficult to imagine any hiring manager getting excited about a candidate because they have phrases like "interpersonal understanding" and "organizational awareness" on their resume.

Like the previous example, this job seeker has a ton of great examples of past successes within the work experience section. Some of these need to be in the professional summary. They would provide the core sales pitch and show the hiring manager how the job seeker will benefit the company.

Example 8: Program Manager

PROGRAM / BUDGET / CONTRACT MANAGER & ANALYST

Extensive leadership experience, including a strong background in the Federal Government Contracting Sector (Department of Defense). Proven success leading numerous multimillion-dollar, large-scale projects on-time and under-budget.

Additional Credentials include: Secret Security Clearance, U.S. Air Force Experience, and MBA

Demonstrated success utilizing problem resolution, analytical and strategic planning skills. Effective leader experienced with building cross-functional teams combining employees and outside contractors to complete complex IT infrastructure and systems projects. Excellent relationship-building skills and capable of driving to consensus with senior executive leaders. Consistently recognized for success throughout military and civilian career.

Assessment: This summary gets off to a great start with the first paragraph. The job seeker provides a clear theme of program management for federal projects. This is followed up with a line about additional credentials. Usually, a line about additional credentials creates a weak presentation. In this case, it really helps because the candidate lists a couple of important elements: military experience and a security clearance. The candidate tried to highlight these, but it looks like he wasn't sure how to best present it. The result was the "Additional Credentials include..." statement. We can simplify this and just list the keywords. For example:

This is more direct and conveys the experience well. There is no need to add a title to the line.

The last paragraph fails to deliver on the good start. It provides a description of a lot of soft skills and makes a very weak impression. This paragraph should be removed, and accomplishments should be added to replace it.

Finally, the title the job seeker uses needs some work. "PROGRAM / BUDGET / CONTRACT MANAGER & ANALYST" is too long. This can be simplified to just Program Manager or Contract Manager. If the candidate wants to broaden this a little, then using "Program Manager/Analyst" would work. It covers two different positions, but stays in the same career field.

Example 9: ERP Consultant

Highlights of Qualifications

- *4+ years experience with ERP software (manufacturing, purchasing, warehousing, project planning, CRM); experience includes implementation, training, technical support and administration.*
- *10+ years of experience developing strong relationships with end-users and providing quality services.*
- *Exceptional project management skills with organizational and problem-solving skills.*
- *Effectively communicates with all levels of the organization regarding ongoing project status reports.*

Assessment: This summary section is short and direct. It has four bullet points focused on the experience level and skills of the job seeker. For an IT consultant, technical knowledge is critical. The candidate leads off with his strength, the technical knowledge he possesses. This is a good approach.

The summary starts with the phrase "Highlights of Qualifications." This generic title misses an opportunity to clearly state the career field the candidate is pursuing. Although the bullet points discuss the candidate's technical knowledge, it isn't until the reader gets into the work experience section that it becomes clear that the job seeker is pursuing an ERP Consulting career. IT is a huge field. Without some indication of the type of work the job seeker is pursuing, the summary section is ineffective. The hiring manager needs to jump to the work experience section to start the assessment.

A summary section needs to stand on its own. If you need to read another part of the resume to understand the summary, then the summary won't work. A reader of a resume needs to understand what job or career field you are pursuing before they can assess anything else. In this example, the job seeker fails to do this.

Additionally, there is nothing in this section demonstrating past success. Adding a few accomplishments would really help. In IT, past accomplishments are typically successful past projects. These also give a good indication of the job seeker's scope of experience.

Finally, the job seeker fails to include any specific ERP packages that he has worked with. There are a number of common ERP packages, and companies often look for IT professionals who have experience with the system they are implementing. Including the specific packages that the job seeker has experience with could help impress hiring managers seeking that experience.

Example 10: Medical Sales Professional

Sales & Business Development Professional

"As a business executive, I often meet with professional sales representatives. <Job Seeker Name> has the traits of top performing sales representatives and exhibits excellent sales skills. I encourage you to consider him for your organization in a sales capacity, and invite you to contact me for further information." <Name of individual providing the quote>

Highly skilled at prospecting, identifying decision-makers, analyzing needs, presenting products, training, negotiating and securing product approvals. Entrepreneurial track record of building and growing a successful business for more than 15 years. Pursuing a career in Medical or Pharmaceutical sales. Highly skilled at driving sales: relationship building, listening, and goal oriented. Open to relocation.

Accomplishments

- *Expanded sales from $50,000 to $680,000 per year.*
- *Exceeded sales goals each year; typically grew annual sales by 10%.*
- *Developed excellent customer loyalty, achieving better than 90% account retention.*

Assessment: This summary section incorporates a quote recommending the job seeker. Although unusual, adding quotes from references is not unheard of. As a tactic on a resume, quotes are not major detractors, but they are unlikely to be major selling points. Anyone can find someone they have worked with who will say something positive about them. In this case, a quote from a random executive is unlikely to do much to further the candidate's chances. What the quote does is focus the reader's attention on assessing the credibility of the person being quoted and the reliability of their assessment of the job seeker. This distracts the reader from the job seeker and focuses attention on the reference.

The rest of the summary is ok. The second paragraph does not flow very well. It's choppy and difficult to read. The sales achievements are good. They provide specific results the job seeker delivered.

Overall, the content of this summary section is good, but there is a lot of non-essential information. A better version would have a couple of sentences summarizing the second paragraph and the accomplishments.

Example 11: New Engineering Graduate

ENGINEERING & MANAGEMENT GRADUATE

Professional Profile

- Analytical and creative with excellent strategic planning skills.
- Resourceful, determined and successful with prospecting and customer presentations.
- Excellent interpersonal, communication, and collaborative relationship-building skills. Energetic, self-motivated, and results-driven.
- Proven leader with demonstrated skill during the successful management of a marketing project team and through positions of increasing responsibility in a social fraternity.
- Comfortable with engineering/technical products and able to communicate effectively to a non-technical audience. Experienced in utilizing personal selling skills.
- Excellent breadth of knowledge and training in engineering and business disciplines.
- Experienced with market research to determine customer needs to properly position a new product during development.
- Conducted due diligence research analyzing a company's strategy, financial condition and industry position to identify recommendations for improvement.

Assessment: This resume comes from a recent college graduate. Recent graduates face the challenge of not having any work experience to highlight. This graduate chose to discuss his skills in his summary. This is a good strategy. A new graduate brings two things to the table – skills and attitude. They don't have experience or past accomplishments. Demonstrating an attitude is very difficult in a resume. Although work ethic, initiative and determination are great characteristics, they are really tough to write about in a way that will be credible. A person's attitude is something that needs to be experienced, and a resume makes it very tough to convey this. Even if a candidate does come up with a good way of describing these attributes, they are unlikely to sound much different from other candidates.

Technical skills are easier to highlight in a resume. This doesn't mean technical skills are more valuable, just that it is often easier to create a strong sales pitch around technical skills than around soft skills and a person's attitude. This job seeker chooses to highlight non-technical skills. It is an interesting choice for someone coming out of an engineering program. The core of an engineering program should be the teaching of technical skills. This is an area the job seeker should be able to highlight well.

New graduates can also highlight what sets them apart. Most graduates worked harder than the minimum requirement needed to graduate. They might have held a leadership position in a school organization, had a high GPA or completed some noteworthy projects in classes. Any of these could be included in a summary statement.

This job seeker chose two of these tactics. He mentions his leadership experience and discusses a class project. Unfortunately, in both cases, he fails to drive home the point. To improve these, he needs to add more detail about what he did. For the leadership bullet, a better description would be "Leadership: Served as Fraternity Vice President for one year and Recruitment Chair for two years. Implemented strategies to boost membership, resulting in a ##% gain in membership." This provides a clear accomplishment and shows the leadership roles the job seeker held.

Example 12: Consultant

EXECUTIVE MANAGEMENT — CONSULTING —
Engineering/Strategic Planning/Product Management

Excellent senior level leader and decision maker, with proven
experience in a multi-national corporate environment. Track
record of developing profitable telecom ventures. Visionary
developer of technology solutions. Proven expert in
marketing, product positioning, technology development
and engineering development.

- *Brought to market a telecom product delivering $45*
  million in sales the first year.

- *Leveraged off-the-shelf components to bypass*
  original development costs estimated at $5,000,000
  during the design and construction of a next-
  generation telecom system.

Assessment: The details of a resume can be distracting and hurt
the overall effectiveness of the resume. This resume illustrates
this. The first line has three keyword phrases. The first two are
capitalized, and the third capitalizes only the first letter of each
word. This is a minor detail. Despite this, a reader of the resume is
likely to spend the next several seconds trying to understand why
the job seeker did this. During this time, the reader is not
concentrating on what they are reading.

There may be a reason the job seeker used capitalization in this
way. The first two phrases refer to types of jobs, and the third
phrase lists different disciplines. Although this may be the

motivation, it still is a distracting feature. If the job seeker wanted to highlight this difference, a good way would be to increase the separation. Grouping the first two phrases and then listing the third phrase would work. For example, "Executive Management/Consulting in Engineering, Strategic Planning or Product Management." This rewrite makes the objective easier to understand. There is still a major problem, and that is the objective is way too broad. The candidate needs to choose an area of focus. Trying to cover two completely different jobs and three completely different disciplines is a mistake.

After the title, the paragraph provides a lot of hype. You should promote yourself in a resume, and a little hype is a good thing. Just remember the claims and hype alone will not get you hired. Lots of job seekers make bold claims. The hype will not set you apart. What will set you apart is how you back up your claims with accomplishments. In a recent resume research study, only 9% of the resumes had any accomplishments listed in the summary section. Adding just one accomplishment to a summary section will help a resume move into the top 10% of all resumes.

The summary section concludes with two accomplishments. Both the accomplishments make a good impression. They relate to new product development, a critical concern in a technology dominated industry like telecom. Although the title and positioning paragraph are unlikely to make a very strong impact, the accomplishments should generate enough interest to motivate a hiring to want to learn more.

Example 13: Marketing Manager

PROFESSIONAL SUMMARY

Seasoned marketing professional with 15+ years of marketing and product management experience in the medical and software industries.

Assessment: This summary is very concise. It conveys the career of the job seeker, the years of experience and the industry background. Overall, this is a fair introduction. It won't make a big impact, but it is short and direct.

The introduction could be expanded an improved with a few small changes. First, changing the title from "Executive Summary" to the job title would help. Second, adding a few accomplishments would provide a more impressive presentation.

Example 14: Construction Manager

OBJECTIVE: Construction Supervisor/Manager utilizing my skills, experience and knowledge for positions offering opportunities for company advancement.

SUMMARY OF QUALIFICATIONS

- *30 years of experience in construction with more than 15 years of experience as a general contractor superintendent.*

- *Proven track record of delivering projects on-time and on-budget.*

- *Extensive knowledge and experience with a full range of residential building products and practices from ground to completion.*

- *Committed to providing high quality work and able to maintain compliance with codes and inspections standards.*

- *Positive professional attitude, committed to excellence, and outstanding work ethic.*

- *Experienced in material and labor estimating, field supervision, problem resolution and inspections.*

- *Managed over 250 construction workers on multiple job sites.*

- *Managed safety and training on job sites.*

- *Excellent organization and documentation skills, with a proven ability to provide detailed tracking of engineering change orders.*

- *Effective in developing cooperative working relationships with sub-contractors, trades people, inspectors, engineers and homeowners.*

Assessment: This summary uses an objective statement followed by a list of bullet points detailing specific experiences. The structure could easily be consolidated by eliminating the objective and replacing "Summary of Qualifications" with "Construction Supervisor/Manager."

The bullet points provide some useful information such as experience managing up to 250 people, but for the most part, the list is uninspiring. It is a list of responsibilities typical of construction managers. Although the job seeker does some boasting, there is nothing to back it up.

In construction, it is common to list major projects. This can be a great tactic to demonstrate the ability of the job seeker. This summary doesn't mention any specific projects. If this job seeker did manage a crew of 250, he must have been on some large jobs. Listing the type of construction, the duration of the project, the size of the project and dollar value of the project can be great additions. Then, adding the result of the project, such as delivering positive budget variances, generating a net profit or beating a deadline, will make a very strong impression.

Example 15: Engineering Ph.D.

RELEVANT EXPERIENCE

- *Ph.D. from the University of <school name>*

- *MS. Eng. and BS. Eng. (with Honors) from the University of <school name>*

- *Extensive knowledge of corrosion, failure analysis, metallurgy and metal fatigue.*

- *40+ publications on corrosion prediction, cyclic corrosion testing methods and underpaint corrosion modeling, including papers in <journal name>; publications cited in research books and papers*

- *Expert with the use of underpaint corrosion simulation and modeling to predict and prevent cathodic delamination. Developed simulation tools for <list of automotive companies>.*

- *Excellent presenter of seminars, lectures, and research work*

- *Past Member of the scientific committee of the <professional society> and referee to technical papers*

Assessment: This is a typical presentation by a researcher. The presentation focuses on the technical expertise and publications of the job seeker. There are no specific financial accomplishments listed. Despite this, the summary is effective. It clearly demonstrates the expertise and industry respect this candidate possesses. A hiring manager seeking a top engineer will look for individuals who provide leadership in their industry. Measuring respectability and leadership in a technical field can be done by assessing the breadth of influence the individual has had. This individual has authored a number of publications. His work has been cited by peers. He has reviewed articles by peers and served in a professional society. We can't tell if this job seeker is at the top of his field, but he is clearly an expert.

The summary section conveys a high level of expertise very well. For many jobs requiring a technical specialist, this may be sufficient. If the company wants a designer who is on the cutting edge of the technology, this resume would warrant an interview. On the other hand, if the company is looking for more than just a pure researcher, this summary section will not be as effective. There is nothing in this summary about minimizing costs or bringing new designs to market. We can't tell if the engineer ever developed a successful product. He may be good at developing interesting theories and ideas that attract the attention of peers in his field, but we can't tell if he is going to successfully develop profitable commercial products. If this is a primary need of the company, the summary section will have missed the mark.

Conclusions

We have looked at a lot of examples from a wide range of industries. Many of the examples provided some value, but most offered significant opportunities for improvement. This is typical of most resumes. The summary section adds a little value but falls well short of the potential for the section.

Improving a professional summary can be accomplished easily. When writing a summary, there is a wide range of structures to choose. One effective structure is starting with a title followed by a short paragraph describing the job seeker's skills, experience and potential, and concluding with a list of accomplishments. This formula works. It is not the only effective way to start a resume, but will provide a great start.

Finally, remember the best practices we reviewed in the previous chapter:

1. Focus your resume on the job you are pursuing. Do not try to be all things to all employers.
2. Be concise. Using fewer words is better. You want to convey your brand and value proposition as quickly as possible and encourage the hiring manager to keep reading.
3. Incorporate accomplishments. Your past successes will do more to sell a hiring manager on your potential than anything else will.
4. Avoid the keyword dump. Listing numerous keywords at the top of your resume will not impress anyone. If something is important enough to be placed at the top of your resume, make sure you explain it.
5. Add titles to your bullet points. Titles are a great way to summarize a bullet point and highlight something in it. This also allows the reader to scan the titles and quickly choose the ones that are most interesting and impressive.

Chapter 13
Customizing Your Resume

To make the strongest sales pitch and demonstrate the potential value you offer, you need to customize your resume for each position you pursue. You cannot use the same resume for every job and expect good results. With every application, you are competing against the best people in the industry. You can compete effectively, but only if you step up to the plate and commit to developing the best presentation of the value you offer every time you send out a resume. This requires customizing your resume for every position.

The first thing to customize on your resume is the title. It's ok to pursue two or three or more different types of jobs at once. It is not ok to generalize your resume for all of them. Be decisive and put a title on the top that applies directly to the position you are applying for. Often this will be a job title or a type of position. Other times, you may use a significant skill that is critical to the position. Regardless of what the title is, make sure it applies directly to the job.

After the title, make sure your description includes the most significant skills and experiences from your background. You will need to change this description for different types of jobs. A skill that is critical in one career may not be as valuable in another. Even within a career field, there will be variations. Focus on skills that are required in the job description. Work to understand the job description and the job as much as possible. The more you learn about the priorities of the company and the hiring manager, the better your customization can be.

Just as you tailor your skills, you need to pick and choose the accomplishments you highlight. You should have a lot of accomplishments to consider including in your resume. Many job seekers struggle with this aspect of resume writing. They can't think of any accomplishments. Usually, this is a result of approaching the problem backwards. They focus on thinking of times when they single handedly delivered a major improvement to the business. Most job seekers do not have the opportunity to do anything single handedly. Organizations are built with teams of employees working together. A better way to identify accomplishments is to focus on your past projects. Make a list of projects, both large and small, where you played some role. List your role and what you did on the project. Then summarize the result of the project.

Choosing which accomplishments to emphasize on your resume is another challenge. If you have done a good job brainstorming about your accomplishments, you will have a long list. You can't put them all in your summary. You need to select the best to highlight. A good accomplishment will demonstrate a contribution you made in the past that would be similar to something the hiring manager would want if you were hired. Look for the accomplishments that most closely relate to the position.

A key factor in choosing the accomplishments you list relates to the needs of the company. The requirements for very similar positions can vary wildly from company to company. There are a number of reasons for this. Consider two direct competitors. Both are manufacturing companies and are seeking production managers. One company implemented Lean Manufacturing five years ago and has been steadily refining their processes. They are committed to manufacturing everything in-house in a single location, with much of their equipment designed and built internally. Another company chose a strategy of outsourcing component manufacturing and assembles products to order. They utilize a number of regional assembly facilities. They are just starting to look at Lean Manufacturing practices and are considering implementing some of them. Both companies could make and sell almost identical products, but the skills and experiences required for a production manager at each company will be vastly different.

To be effective, you must choose accomplishments that are similar to the job and company you are seeking. This is incredibly important, but not the only criteria for selecting a good accomplishment for the summary section. There are times when the most effective accomplishment isn't the biggest or most directly related to the job. It is critical that you choose accomplishments that can be communicated easily. You may have led a project that saved $10 million, but a project saving $100k may be more impressive at the top of your resume.

The key to an accomplishment being impressive on a resume is often determined by the clarity of the description. Very complex projects that require extensive explanations don't work well on a resume. The best accomplishments will be simple and easy to understand. Your resume is going to be read by a variety of people, and many will not be technical experts in your field. An HR Manager might understand the basics of what you do, but is unlikely to possess a high level of technical expertise in your field. Keeping your examples short and simple will greatly improve the impression you make.

You need a two-step solution to this dilemma. First, you need to research the company, facility and position thoroughly. If you don't know how they operate, you can't tailor your sales pitch to their needs. Second, you need to customize your resume to lead with your best sales pitch. You might have a dozen accomplishments, each related to different challenges and skills that you can highlight on your resume. When you identify the requirements of the position, you should select the accomplishments that best suit the priorities of that company.

For example, consider a candidate seeking either an account management position or an applications engineer position. For the account management position, the candidate needs to emphasize his past success in sales. This will include examples of major accounts opened, a track record of beating sales quotas and his success of growing sales year over year. The accomplishments for sales will be relatively straightforward.

The role of an applications engineer will be a little more challenging to find the right accomplishments. This is a sales support function requiring a high level of technical expertise. The role is not responsible for generating new sales or closing sales independently, but instead helps sales reps close deals. The accomplishments will need to reflect this. They will focus on improving closing ratios and supporting overall sales growth for the team. In addition to these accomplishments, a few individual sales accomplishments would be good to include as well. Although the role is a sales support role, there is a significant sales component to it. The result is a combination of accomplishments for individual sales and team sales support.

Even if you use the same accomplishment for multiple positions, you may still need to tailor the accomplishment. Most achievements require a variety of skills and activities. They also can have a variety of benefits. What you emphasize in the accomplishment is as important what you accomplished.

Consider the production manager from our earlier example. The candidate has great lean manufacturing experience, but only one of his target companies has embraced lean. The other company isn't looking for a lean expert. Now consider the following accomplishment:

- ***Implemented Lean****: Led the Lean Implementation as the manufacturing manager of a Tier 1 automotive plant with responsibility for over 800 production workers and supervisors. Completed the implementation over a two-year time period, resulting in a 60% reduction in lead times and a 25% improvement in productivity.*

This is a great accomplishment for the company embracing lean manufacturing, but for the other company, it won't work as well. They just aren't interested in lean, and the hiring manager may not even read the accomplishment due to the title. Fortunately, we can rewrite this to fit the second company.

- ***Improved Productivity 25%****: Implemented process improvements that cut lead times and improved productivity as the manufacturing manager of a Tier 1 automotive plant with responsibility for over 800 production workers and supervisors, resulting in a 60% reduction in lead times and a 25% improvement in productivity.*

This version provides identical information as the previous version, but deemphasizes the lean implementation and focuses more on individual techniques and results achieved.

Look for ways to tailor your resume to the position and the company you are pursuing. You will maximize your chances for success if you develop a targeted resume for each position instead of using a generic version for every job.

Chapter 14
Formatting a Professional Summary

The content and structure of your professional summary are critical to its effectiveness. Without good content and organization, no amount of formatting will be able to save your resume. Once you get the content and structure right, then you can maximize the effectiveness by improving the formatting. There are a few easy to implement techniques you can use to improve your professional summary.

Alignment

The bulk of your resume should be left aligned. Hiring managers scanning your resume will follow the left edge of the resume from top to bottom looking for the most important information. This is natural. We read from left to right, so people are trained to look left first. You do not need to align everything to the left, though.

You want a hiring manager to read your professional summary first, but it isn't the first thing listed on your resume. Your name and contact information will be at the top of your resume, above the professional summary.

Most job seekers place their name and contact information on the top left or top center of the resume. These positions will naturally draw the reader's attention first. There is nothing wrong with this, but you have a short window to capture the reader's attention. Your name, unless you are a well-known celebrity or personally know the hiring manager, is unlikely to impress anyone. It is a portion of your resume that is essential, but not valuable for assessing your potential.

You can deemphasize your name and contact information by right aligning them. Shifting them to the right side of the page will place the title of your summary section as the first thing on the left. It will draw the reader to your professional summary before reading anything else.

Font Size

The professional summary is designed to be your strongest presentation of your potential. You want to emphasize it and show that it is more important than the rest of the resume. You do this by placing it at the top of the resume, but you can use the font size to reinforce that the summary section is important and needs to be read. Consider choosing a font size one or two points larger than the size of the main text of your resume. This will help to set it off from the rest of the resume and provide more emphasis.

Be careful with this technique. There are times when increasing the font size of the summary section turns a really good looking resume into an unattractive one. There is no rule on this. It's a matter of style and personal taste. Try modifying the font size and see how it works.

Bold

Using bold text can help draw attention to titles and other significant elements. Most job seekers use a lot of bold text. Some go too far and find a reason to bold almost everything. The more you use bold text, the less significance it will convey. Try to keep your bolding to a minimum and use it to really emphasize a few key titles.

Italics

Italicized text is more difficult to read on a computer screen. For resumes in print, it's not bad. Generally, you should minimize italics and use it only for elements you want to differentiate from other text. In your professional summary, you want to keep it short, concise and full of impact. Because computer monitors have more trouble rendering italics accurately, you may cause people to avoid italicized text that you want to emphasize. It is safer to avoid italics in your professional summary. The computer screen resolution also affects the choice of fonts. Serif fonts like New Times Roman look great in print but are tougher to read on a screen. San Serif fonts like Arial are easier to read on a screen but lose out in print. Because most resumes are read on a screen and not in print, you are better off sticking to a san serif font and avoiding italics.

All Caps

Placing text in all capital letters will draw attention to the text. The capitals are larger than regular text and offer a way to increase the size of a phrase without changing the font size. The capitalized text will also draw the reader's attention. Using all caps can be a great way to emphasize an important element. Like the other formatting techniques, use all caps in moderation. Placing too much text in all caps will dilute the effect and hurt the effectiveness of the resume.

Bullets and Indenting

Indents are a great tool to provide structure to a resume. They are especially helpful in the work experience section. The professional summary section can benefit from indenting as well. Accomplishments are so critical that you want to make sure hiring managers read them. A great way to do this is to put your accomplishments in a bulleted list and indent the list in from the margin. This sets the list off from the rest of the professional summary. Most people will be drawn to the bullets and the indented text. They naturally will assume the bullets provide the most important information. Use this to your advantage and put your best selling points in an indented bulleted list in your professional summary.

Chapter 15
Choosing the Right Verbs

Selecting the right verbs to make the strongest impact can be difficult. To help with this process, some of the better verbs for resumes are listed below.

Abolished	Conducted	Examined
Accelerated	Constructed	Exceeded
Accomplished	Convinced	Expanded
Achieved	Coordinated	Expedited
Acted	Created	Fabricated
Adapted	Debugged	Financed
Added	Decreased	Focused
Adopted	Delivered	Formed
Advanced	Demonstrated	Formulated
Amplified	Determined	Founded
Analyzed	Developed	Fulfilled
Applied	Directed	Furnished
Automated	Discovered	Gained
Awarded	Earned	Generated
Benchmarked	Eliminated	Hired
Bolstered	Enabled	Identified
Boosted	Encouraged	Illustrated
Captured	Engineered	Implemented
Changed	Enhanced	Improved
Coached	Enlarged	Incorporated
Combined	Enriched	Increased
Communicated	Established	Initiated

Innovated	Prepared	Solved
Instigated	Prevented	Spearheaded
Integrated	Procured	Specified
Introduced	Proposed	Stabilized
Invented	Provided	Standardized
Judged	Purchased	Steered
Justified	Quantified	Strategized
Launched	Raised	Streamlined
Led	Received	Strengthened
Liquidated	Recommended	Structured
Maintained	Recovered	Supervised
Managed	Recruited	Surpassed
Mapped	Redesigned	Tailored
Marketed	Reduced	Targeted
Maximized	Refined	Trained
Merged	Regained	Transformed
Minimized	Rejected	Troubleshot
Modeled	Reorganized	Uncovered
Modernized	Repaired	Undertook
Modified	Replaced	Updated
Motivated	Resolved	Upgraded
Netted	Restored	Utilized
Obtained	Restructured	Validated
Operated	Resulted	Verified
Orchestrated	Revamped	Won
Organized	Reversed	Yielded
Originated	Revitalized	
Partnered	Salvaged	
Pinpointed	Secured	
Pioneered	Shaped	
Planned	Simplified	

Chapter 16
Choosing the Right Adjectives

Selecting the right adjectives to describe your experiences and accomplishments is a challenge. To help with this process, some of the better adjectives for resumes are listed below.

Abounding	Capable	Deeply
Acceptable	Careful	Delicate
Accurate	Cautious	Dependent
Adaptable	Certain	Detailed
Aggressive	Changeable	Determined
Agreeable	Clean	Difficult
Amazing	Clear	Diligent
Ambitious	Clever	Disastrous
Aspiring	Colossal	Distinct
Astonishing	Complete	Divergent
Auspicious	Complex	Dynamic
Automatic	Cooperative	Eager
Average	Coordinated	Early
Awesome	Courageous	Easy
Beneficial	Cumbersome	Economic
Best	Curious	Effective
Better	Cut	Efficient
Big	Damaged	Elated
Bite-Sized	Damaging	Electric
Black-And-White	Dangerous	Eminent
Boundless	Dazzling	Empty
Bustling	Dead	Encouraging
Calculating	Decisive	Energetic
Calm	Deep	Enormous

Enthusiastic	Inquisitive	Possible
Excited	Instinctive	Powerful
Exciting	Intelligent	Premium
Exclusive	Judicious	Previous
Expensive	Knowledgeable	Probable
Fabulous	Large	Productive
Fair	Little	Quick
Fantastic	Long-Term	Rampant
Fast	Low	Rapid
Fearless	Maddening	Rare
Few	Magnificent	Ready
Fine	Massive	Remarkable
First	Marvelous	Resonant
Fixed	Mere	Right
Flawless	Mighty	Selective
Fortunate	Miniature	Serious
Frequent	Minor	Shocking
Functional	Modern	Simple
Futuristic	Momentous	Simplistic
Giant	Near	Skillful
Gigantic	Necessary	Smart
Good	Needless	Steadfast
Great	Normal	Steady
Handy	Numerous	Strong
Helpful	Obtainable	Stupendous
High	Old	Substantial
Hot	Onerous	Successful
Huge	Opposite	Sudden
Hulking	Optimal	Super
Immense	Ordinary	Superb
Important	Outstanding	Supreme
Imported	Overrated	Swift
Impossible	Painstaking	Talented
Industrious	Pathetic	Tangible
Incredible	Perfect	Temporary
Inexpensive	Perpetual	Tenuous

Terrible	Ultra	Wasteful
Terrific	Understood	Wonderful
Tested	Unequaled	Workable
Tremendous	Utmost	Yielding
Troubled	Valuable	
Typical	Vast	

Other Books By Palladian

Resume Writing for Manufacturing Careers, Gary W. Capone, 2010

In a very competitive manufacturing job market, this book is the tool you need to write a more effective resume that gets results. It is customized to the needs of manufacturing professionals, with detailed examples, all tailored to manufacturing careers. The examples illustrate common mistakes and the ways to correct them. The book shows a systematic process for writing and improving a resume, and then illustrates this process in a comprehensive, step-by-step example. The example, covered over six chapters, shows the resume writing process of a hypothetic manufacturing professional in great detail. Two incredibly powerful tools vital to your success are included with the book. The Resume Assessment shows you how to assess your finished resume. Each of the 30 assessment steps includes a short best practice explanation. The Work Experience Worksheet is a tool to help you collect the data you need to write your resume and find the career features that give you an edge over your competition. With these tools, the detailed examples and the techniques taught in the book, you will gain the knowledge you need to develop a resume to impress hiring managers and get more interviews.

Power Up Your Job Search: A Modern Approach to Interview Preparation, Gary W. Capone and Mark Henderson, 2009

The Power Up Approach to Interview Preparation simplifies the interview prep process into a series of quick, easy and effective steps. The approach incorporates powerful techniques proven to be effective. The Power Up Approach will benefit job seekers at all levels, including new graduates just entering the workforce, professionals looking for the next step in their career, transitioning military personnel and seasoned executives. This book will give you the tools you need to sell your potential to an employer, through a series of lessons, each packed full of advice, techniques and exercises. For many professionals, following our approach will give them a distinct advantage over the competition.

Made in the USA
Charleston, SC
09 February 2012